mmunity College

FIND OUT ABOUT—

- Your child's elaborate, sometimes amusing, often exasperating rituals. Should you go along with them? *See page 13.*

- Time with a baby-sitter—why it's a great idea for your Two-year-old . . . and for you! *See page 14.*

- Hitting, pushing, grabbing, and other aggressive acts: Is this normal Two-year-old behavior . . . or time for a parent to take action. *See pages 20–21.*

- Step-by-step parenting tips that work. Discover sixteen sure-fire things to do to make the "Terrible Twos" a terrific year. *See pages 38–39.*

- A warning you might not expect. Why you *should not* try to teach your Two-year-old to read. *See page 57.*

- Toilet training . . . with no more tears. Why a set of little steps placed close to the toilet and other simple remedies—even for persistent problems—will make it easy. *See pages 82–84.*

. . . and more!

YOUR TWO-YEAR-OLD

"I think [these books] are delightful and likely to capture the imagination of young parents enough to get them through these years. . . . I think the books will be both a pleasure and support for many parents."

—T. Berry Brazelton, M.D., author of
Toddlers and Parents and *Infants and Mothers*

"These are cheerful, optimistic books. . . . I agree with just about everything they say."

—Lendon Smith, M.D., author of
Feed Your Kids Right

Books from the Gesell Institute of Human Development

YOUR ONE-YEAR-OLD
Ames, Ilg, and Haber

YOUR TWO-YEAR-OLD
Ames and Ilg

YOUR THREE-YEAR-OLD
Ames and Ilg

YOUR FOUR-YEAR-OLD
Ames and Ilg

YOUR FIVE-YEAR-OLD
Ames and Ilg

YOUR SIX-YEAR-OLD
Ames and Ilg

YOUR SEVEN-YEAR-OLD
Ames and Haber

YOUR EIGHT-YEAR-OLD
Ames and Haber

YOUR NINE-YEAR-OLD
Ames and Haber

YOUR TEN- TO FOURTEEN-YEAR-OLD
Ames, Ilg, and Haber

your TWO-YEAR-OLD

Terrible or Tender

by Louise Bates Ames, Ph.D.
and Frances L. Ilg, M.D.
Gesell Institute of Human Development

Illustrated with photographs

A DELL TRADE PAPERBACK

To our daughters,
Joan and Tordis,

and our grandchildren,
Carol, Clifford, Karl, and Whittier

P94179

CONTENTS

chapter one
ARE THOSE TWOS REALLY SO TERRIBLE?

Your Two-year-old! Different in many ways from any other living human being! And yet, because the individual boy or girl does develop to a large extent in a patterned, predictable way, there are many respects in which he or she will resemble every other Two-year-old.

Only you will fully and intimately know your own preschooler. But because he will resemble others of his same age in so many ways, there is much we can tell you about Two-year-oldness in general that should provide something of a shortcut to your understanding and appreciation of that young person who is so uniquely your own.

The child of this age has come a long way when compared with his own Eighteen- to Twenty-one-month-old self. We have described the Eighteen-month-old as walking along a one-way street that all too often leads in the opposite direction from the one you had in mind. He bumbles along in his own peculiar way and almost seems to think with his feet. As one perceptive mother remarked of her own Eighteen-month-old, "You program him just as if he were a computer—he is that predictable."

Predictable, perhaps, to others but not always to himself. His abilities are still so rudimentary that his life holds all too many unhappy surprises. He falls when he wants to stay upright. Things slip from his hands when he wishes to

1

He lacks the words he needs to express his very d definite demands.

ↄ...s lack of abilities all too often upsets him. He is upset with himself and with his parents. Life is by no means entirely smooth or happy.

Hence it may come as a pleasant relief to all concerned when the Eighteen- to Twenty-one-month-old boy or girl turns Two, and at least briefly things go more to his liking and to your own.

The typical Two-year-old tends to be a rather gentle, friendly little person, much, much easier to live with than he was a mere few months ago. One of the reasons for this is that life is easier for him now than it used to be.

To begin with, he is much more sure of himself motorwise than he was just a few months ago. Now he can walk and run and climb with rather admirable skill, so the world of movement is a comfortable one for him.

Now he can talk so much better than he could at Eighteen or Twenty-one months. Not only can he express his needs much better, but since Two is a somewhat relaxed, undemanding age, these needs are not so strong as they used to be. This happy combination—less vigorous demands and a much better ability to express them—makes it easier for the child to get what he wants from the world.

Emotionally he seems calmer, surer, better balanced than he was. Anger and disappointment are not as strongly felt as formerly, nor are they as strongly expressed. He is happy much of the time. He likes other people, and they, in turn, find him a delightful companion.

A few months earlier, the child seemed to favor an extensor posture. If you tried to take him onto your lap, he would, as likely as not, straighten out and slide down. Now, if you catch him in just the right mood, he may curl up and settle in, and talk to you or merely listen.

Two expresses affection warmly. He enjoys you, and you enjoy him. Gone is the difficult, demanding little boy or girl with whom you may have suffered just a few short months ago.

The age of Two usually provides a brief and welcome breathing space for a parent, coming as it does between the difficult, demanding time of Eighteen to Twenty-one months and the even more difficult and demanding age of Two-and-a-half that is so soon to follow. In fact, the year begins so gently that one is not at first aware of the hidden sources of dominating power that will be unleashed in its midstream.

You as a parent may not feel that you need a tremendous amount of help in living with this delightful little creature. Our suggestion is, Enjoy any periods of calm, of equilibrium, of contentment, of comfort while they last, for in many children, especially during the preschool years, they tend to be rather short. In these early years one finds that most harmonious stages, when the child seems to be in tune with Nature, comfortable with himself and happy with you, easy to deal with and to live with, tend to be rather brief.

"The Terrible Twos" is a phrase that has become a part of our culture. This phrase is not entirely correct. Any parent of a friendly, amenable Two-year-old is bound to consider it a definite exaggeration.

Yet, as your child moves on through this year that begins with his second birthday (actually the third year of his life), you will discover, all too soon, what people are talking about. The gentle age of Two is all too quickly followed by the age of Two-and-a-half, when things are not so gentle. Thus one should say more accurately, "The Gentle Twos." It is not until Two-and-a-half that many children do become rather terrible. It is Two-and-a-half, not Two itself, that gives this general age period such a very bad name.

It is as if the child could not function always on the positive side of life. Stages, or ages, when things are fine and in good equilibrium, seem to need to break up and to be followed by stages when things are not so fine and equilibrium is not so steady.

We call this manner of growing *interweaving* (*see* Figure 1). *Good* seems to need to interweave with *bad*; *equilibrium* with *disequilibrium*. The good, solid equilibrium of any early age seems to need to *break up* into disequilibrium before the child can reach a higher or more mature stage of equilibrium, which again will be followed by disequilibrium. But take heart. As day follows night, so equilibrium will again return.

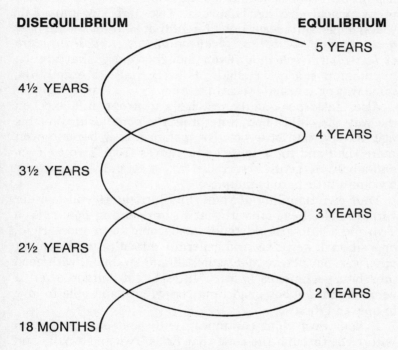

DISEQUILIBRIUM

EQUILIBRIUM

5 YEARS

4½ YEARS

4 YEARS

3½ YEARS

3 YEARS

2½ YEARS

2 YEARS

18 MONTHS

Figure 1
Alternation of Ages of Equilibrium and Disequilibrium

Almost invariably, as your Two-year-old matures, he reaches the not entirely comfortable stage of Two-and-a-half. And since it is at the stages of disequilibrium that the parent or other person who is taking care of the child needs most help, we shall write somewhat briefly of Two, and will give you all the help we can with Two-and-a-half.

SPECIAL WARNING

Remember—please remember—that every child not only has his own individuality—even identical twins differ from each other in many important ways—but each also has his own time schedule. We describe here ways in which many typical children behave at Two and Two-and-a-half years of age. But please don't forget that *your own child may quite normally be behind or ahead of this supposedly more or less typical schedule.* Even though children have much in common, not every child hits every stage in exactly the same way or at exactly the same time.

Also, basic personality will have a strong influence on the way the child's body interprets the complexities of this age. A very rigid little boy, for instance, may become even more rigid and intractable as he moves from Two to Two-and-a-half. A gentle, tractable girl may only temporarily become a little hard to manage.

Your own handling of your child introduces still another variable. Met head-on with harsh, unrelenting demands, a Two-and-a-half-year-old tends to become even more rigid, oppositional, negative, and generally difficult than he might otherwise have been. Met with skill and kindness, with good preschool techniques, with a little bit of humor, even a very demanding boy or girl may be willing and able to give in now and then.

If your own child continues gentle and easy to get on with right through the time that he is Two-and-a-half, and does not reach the terrible Two-and-a-half period until he is almost Three, don't be alarmed. And if because by nature he is just naturally calm and adaptable, and because your own handling may be superb, he is not ever very terrible at any time during this third year, don't worry about that, either.

Don't worry about it, but don't credit all of this smoothness to your own handling. His younger brother or sister, when he or she comes along, may be very different.

And if our description of Two-and-a-half-year-old behavior

makes that entire age period seem like a disaster area, it
isn't necessarily so. Even the Two-and-a-half-year-old can
be as delightful at times as any other preschooler. He is
often very lovable, engaging, enthusiastic, and appreciative.
It is interesting, though, that often the stubborn, aggressive
side of the Two-and-a-half-year-old's nature surfaces again
when he becomes a teenager—moody, petulant, and all-
too-ready to criticize you as a parent.

Fortunately, for all his rebelling, his stubborn opposition,
even the Two-and-a-half-year-old still believes that **you**,
his parents, are all-powerful and all-wonderful.

The hints, techniques, and warnings that we are about
to give you are meant to help you keep things on as smooth
a track as possible so that you and your child can most fully
enjoy each other while the complex and exquisite process
of maturing is going on.

chapter two
GENERAL CHARACTERISTICS OF THE AGE

THE TWO-YEAR-OLD

For many parents, Two is the best age of all. The Two-year-old has finally emerged from his impulsive, thrusting, bumbling Eighteen-month-old ways. Gone are the days when he saw nothing to the right or left of him but went straight to his goal, plowing through anything in his way. Then he needed the protective, restraining help of his parents to break his fall, to teach him about danger.

The Two-year-old has also emerged from his Twenty-one-month-old ways, when he tried to be his own protector, when he froze in his own tracks, often from fear. Then he needed reassurance from his parents. With their help he unfroze and grew warm in their loving, understanding care of him. Gradually he clung less and grew more independent. Above all, as he approached Two, he grew more deeply in love with his parents, who became "my mommy" and "my daddy."

Emotionally, Two seems much of the time to be comfortable and content. Life feels good to him. Emotions do not take over as they do at some other ages. Two can express his warm affections both by the sound of his voice and by his cozy, snuggling ways. There is an easy give-and-take between parent and child. *He now seems comfortable with himself*. He speaks of himself by his given name, usually coupled with some demand: "Johnny wants a cookie," "Mary wants go go outside." He not only expresses his desires, but he wishes to possess, to have things all his own. The air may ring with the often repeated refrain, "It's mine. It's mine." And this is quite fair, since a child must first learn "mine" before he can appreciate "thine."

What a delightful companion he can be in the home! He moves around the house with increasing ease. He goes on little errands. His favorite errand may be the fetching of Daddy's slippers at the end of the day. He loves to go out for a walk and to walk on the tops of low walls. But he always loves to come "home again."

The world around him is pouring in through his eyes,

and he remembers much of what he sees. He knows where things go. He dotes on putting away the canned goods. He loves to watch all household activities—the vacuuming of the floor, the making of beds, the beating of eggs, and especially the scrubbing of the bathroom. He is beginning to take a hand in all of these activities himself. He delights in imitating and enjoys working side by side with his mother, using his own miniature equipment.

Whatever attracts him (and almost everything does) he approaches and touches, prolonging or repeating the sensory experience until he has had his fill. And he explores not only by touch but by taste and smell as well. He still has almost everything to learn, and he is learning very quickly. That is why it is so important not to have dangerous medicines and cleaning fluids within his reach.

He cannot yet be given the run of the house, for he still tends to produce his own special kind of havoc—he gets into his mother's powders and creams; he strews and he smears. Doors need to be equipped with high hooks now that he can turn doorknobs so deftly. His easy access to the bathroom, however, is often very rewarding. Those children who have not yet been toilet trained (for either bowel or bladder) often suddenly train themselves in a mere week's time. (This success is greatly facilitated by the use of a potty chair.) Water play quiets and intrigues as no other play at Two. A strong and steady stool is needed so the child can reach the washbasin.

Two likes the feeling of having the same thing happen day after day. Routine suits him. "Again" is an oft-repeated demand. In the morning he likes having his bedroom slippers and bathrobe put on and then going in to watch his daddy shave. The sequence is important. The evening has its own special sequence, too, often including his favorite "bookie." Books that he might enjoy at this time may be the *Golden Dictionary* or *Goodnight Moon*.

Even in eating he is beginning to enjoy repetition. Thus, his diet, even though adequate, may be restricted. He feeds himself the things he likes best, though still with considerable spilling. Often he eats best alone, calling his mother when he is "ready" for the next course. One really good meal a day may be all that can be expected of him.

His typical day involves much simple exploration and investigation.

THE TWO-AND-A-HALF-YEAR-OLD

Life can be so smooth and delightful with the Two-year-old that it may be quite a jolt when he turns Two-and-a-half and all too often becomes tense, explosive, and rigid. Two, in many boys and girls, is an age of rather straightforward, sure, uncomplicated functioning. Two-and-a-half can be a time of difficulty in many ways, and especially difficult when violent, demanding, explosive emotions take over, as they so often do.

Most of all, one feels that this is a time of opposite extremes. By his very nature, the child of this age has merely to choose the *red* one, and he wants the *blue*; to choose *yes*, and he definitely wishes *no*.

At Eighteen months, the typical boy or girl walks down a one-way street, and his direction tends to be the *opposite* of the way *you* have directed. Now he has matured to the point where he sets up his own opposites. This is how he finds out about the world—by exploring *both* of any two opposite extremes in quick succession. Annoying as this kind of behavior may be to the adult, it is a very important part of growing up. Soon will come the time when he *can* make a choice and stick to it.

A second striking characteristic of the Two-and-a-half-year-old is his demand for sameness. He wants everything to always be the same. It is not just the order in which things are carried out, or the way they are done that must be the same. It is the place they occupy. He wants everything in the household to stay right where he put it or where he thinks it belongs. And, he wants everything to be *appropriate*—belongings to go with the people they *belong* to. If a

visitor borrows, and wears, his mother's sweater, for instance, this may be quite upsetting to him. (The child shows a need for sameness, and yet he does like to explore and investigate.)

The child himself fulfills his need for sameness by setting up elaborate, sometimes amusing, sometimes exasperating rituals to keep himself on the right track. The rituals help him avoid the conflict of having to make a choice. He may even have a dressing ritual (which Father had better learn about before he tries to help out in the morning). Putting on shirt before pants when he wants his pants put on before his shirt may be an adequate reason for having a temper tantrum.

Some of his rituals take a very long time, and if not followed correctly may have to be gone through all over again from the beginning. Such rituals can be a tyranny. One little girl insisted on putting fifteen dolls to bed every night. (Half a dozen dolls might have been quite enough for her and could have simplified her ritual.)

His sense of place may extend to an insistence on always taking exactly the same route to nursery school or to some other familiar destination. The world is large and confusing to the child of this age. A consistent route helps orient him and gives him confidence.

Time, too, must be programmed for him to feel comfortable. If Father usually comes home just before supper, and on one particular day comes home early, your Two-and-a-half-year-old will still expect supper to follow immediately after Father's appearance. His time tends to be *event* time, not clock time.

In fact, speaking of Father's appearance, some children at this age are so extremely programmed that if Father comes in a different door from usual, it can be upsetting. As one such child interpreted it: "Daddy come in front door. One daddy. Daddy come in the back door. Two daddies."

Soon will come the day, probably when your child is nearing Three, that he will be so secure within himself that he will not need the support of an environment that stays always the same. He will be able to permit variety, to accept the new as well as the tried and the true. But now he seems to bolster up his not-very-secure sense of self with a demand for everything to stay just the same.

This is possibly the worst age of any for making choices. Two-and-a-half vacillates back and forth, and if he finally settles for one of two choices, he is almost bound to choose the other immediately. Thus, the simple choice between chocolate or vanilla cookies may ruin an excursion to the store. Possibly it is better that he stay at home so that this kind of problem, so difficult to solve, will not arise.

This is an age when conflict with the parent may be so extreme and frequent that it may be wise for someone other than the parent to take over, at least for part of the time. Some extra money for a baby-sitter could be set aside. But with the cost of baby-sitters an added burden, parents in some communities are now helping each other out for short periods of time, perhaps an hour or two. Some parents of Two-year-olds are even forming small groups, say of four children, who go to each others' houses twice a week for perhaps two hours, with two mothers in attendance. And fortunate is the child who has a grandmother or aunt living nearby!

Nursery school is also a possibility. Some Two-year-olds may do best if an arrangement is made so that mothers can stay for the entire school period, though most Two-and-a-half-year-olds can manage nursery school by themselves, without Mother in attendance.

The Two-and-a-half-year-old may be, above all else, imperious, bossy, and demanding, to the extent that mothers often nickname their child "King John" or "Queen Marie." But it helps to remember that the child is bossy not because he is sure, but actually because he is unsure. The world still seems big and dangerous to him. If he can command even a small part of it (his parents), it helps him to feel secure.

This tends to be an age of exaggerated tensional outlets. Thumb sucking increases; stuttering may appear temporarily, especially with the very talkative child. He may scream and produce a temper tantrum on the tiniest provocation. Your once-enchanting Two-year-old has now become a demon or, as noted above, a complete despot. If advanced, he has discovered the pronoun "I"; otherwise he calls himself "me." Thus, he proclaims, "I need," "I want," or, "Me can do it!"

"No" is another much-used word, and its use is increased if you unwittingly ask a question that can be answered in the negative. Safer to make an entirely positive statement to him: "It's time to——," "You need to——." This allows less opportunity for royal rebellion than would an unwise question.

Clearly, the child of this age is handicapped by an almost total inability to modulate. He is made up of extremes. As we've said before, this is part and parcel of the growth process. So, he is exuberant one minute, shy the next. He says, "Me do it myself," when he can't do a thing, and, "You do it," when he can. He clamors for a special food one minute, rejects it the next. He insists on feeding himself at one meal; then, often when his mother is busiest, demands complete help. He is keen to possess a certain object, snatching it from another child; is indifferent to it when it is once possessed. The grass is always greener, for him, in someone else's pasture. He acts with sudden speed or dawdles endlessly.

He may disrupt parental harmony by pitting Mother against Father. And he can drive everyone to distraction by his insistence that "Mommy do it" when Daddy is taking over, and then that "Daddy do it" when Mommy takes hold. In fact, his insistent "Mommy do" when Dad is helping out is often a cause for hurt feelings. It shouldn't be. The person he wants is *whatever* person is not available at the moment, and if everyone *is* available, his demand may change to "Me do it myself." (Though when he is really in trouble, it is nearly always Mommy whom he wants.)

However, we must take care not to malign the Two-and-a-half-year-old. For all his rigidities and complexities, much of the time he can be a delightful companion for his parents and for other grown-ups. Say he doesn't want to share any of his toys with other children—and much of the time he doesn't—if you look on his behavior as emerging and not just as selfish or naughty, it can be fun to help him, with your own techniques, to come to the point where he can at least *begin* to share.

If he demands that his bedtime book be read "again, and again, and again" (to use his own words), it can be fun to help him to the point where you can bargain and can limit.

If he bugs you with an incessant "Why?" every time you give a command, it can be fun to support him toward the points where "Why?" is a request for information and not merely a word of resistance.

Everything is still very new to him, and it is fun to show him new things, tell him new facts, share his unfolding emotions. It is even more fun to watch him as he manipulates his way toward getting the things he wants. Thus, a child of this age, whose television viewing has been restricted, may ask a visiting relative, "Aunt Weese—want to watch television?" If his aunt says "Yes," he may then go to his parent, in another room, and report, "Aunt Weese wants to watch television."

He is, in fact, often a good deal more wily than the adult realizes, and with his increasing vocabulary and his vast and enthusiastic interest in everything that happens, he is often putting two and two together to a far greater extent than one's casual observation may make evident.

And, when things go well, he is, above all, so appreciative and so loving that it can be a treat to spend time in his company.

At any rate, it is no wonder, after all the tension and all the demands that characterize the age period of Two-and-a-half, that a period of exhaustion should follow. As the child moves on toward Three, he may seem to get tired easily. He may complain that he is sleepy and want to be carried. If you go on a walk without his stroller, even though he may reject it imperiously when you start out,

you're likely to end up carrying a drowsy, heavy child who can't walk any farther.

Whining is one expression of this fatigue. The child not only feels like a baby but wants to act like one, at least part of the time. As one little girl of this age expressed it, "I'm a little baby. I can't walk. And I drink from my bottle. But I *can* talk."

The Two-and-a-half-year-old child not only acts like a baby but he loves to hear about his babyhood. As he moves on toward Three, it sometimes seems as though he cannot hear enough about himself as a baby. He likes to hear about what he wore, how he cried, where he slept, how he was fed. Most of all, he likes to be told, "And you were the best baby there ever was."

The boy or girl of this age, like his just earlier self, becomes very easily *frustrated*. Almost any restriction of his bodily movements is hard for him to accept, especially when it keeps him from doing something that he wants to do. His own lack of skill also frustrates him when the things he is making with his hands so often don't turn out as he expects.

Interruptions to his play—which, of course, come often in daily life—are very real frustrations for him. It may seem to the child that play is constantly interrupted by parental demands that he eat, sleep, go to the bathroom, come into the house. And play with other children inevitably brings its own frustrations, since other children, even like himself, tend to grab, snatch, refuse to share, or to play as he wants them to play.

Yes, life offers many frustrations for the Two-and-a-half-year-old, and, in spite of a mother's and father's best efforts, some temper and some tantrums will occur.

chapter three
THE CHILD WITH OTHER CHILDREN

THE TWO-YEAR-OLD

The Two-year-old (unlike the Two-and-a-half-year-old, who becomes so easily frustrated) does enjoy the company of other children, but often so gently, so minimally that one might wonder if the opportunity of being with others is really worthwhile. We are sure that it is. Just because there is not a great deal of interaction does not mean that the child is not enjoying the situation and benefiting from it.

Any play group tends to be extremely quiet, often giving the impression that not much is going on, and what movement there is may be rather slow.

Experienced adults already know, and others soon discover, that the outstanding characteristic of social life at this age is what is known as *parallel play*. Children in a group may at first play in all different parts of the room. But soon the more social gather—sometimes only two, sometimes three or more—around some simple, undemanding focus.

Thus, two or three children may play, separately, with little pegboards placed on a table. Several may play, though in an extremely rudimentary way, with bits of Play-Doh, all at the same table. Several may gather around a sandbox, each scooping up his own sand. That is, they may all be doing more or less the same thing, and playing with more or less the same kind of material, and may all be in much the same place, but without much interaction.

Gradually one may look at another, or several may stare warily at each other. Soon one child may smile at another, and, before long, as the days go by, one may start to talk to another. This "talk" may consist merely of saying the other child's name repetitively: "Sandy, Sandy." It may be a mere social greeting: "Hi," "Hello." It may be calling attention to the child's own accomplishment. It may be a complaint, as when somebody pulls a girl's hair and she says, "Hurts." But the most common word uttered is usually "Mine," as the child tries to protect his possessions from everybody else.

Often each child seems to pursue his own way with very little regard for any of the others. But if some center of interest is emphasized by an adult, the children may not seem to want to be left out of any physical group, and there may be a mass drift to a guinea pig cage or to the clay table or to the phonograph. Children drift together, and then they drift apart.

It is very important for any socially ambitious mother or teacher of a Two-year-old to appreciate that sociality will probably not go much beyond all this. It is also important to remember that children of this age quite naturally engage in a good deal of physical exploration of each other. Hitting at this age does not necessarily mean dislike. It may be the one form of social contact the child knows best. Or, a child may begin by stroking another child's hair because he likes the way it looks, then may pull it to see how it feels.

It is by no means unusual for a child to grab an object from another child, to chase and shout for an object, to push a child out of the way and then grab something, or to hit another child on the head and then climb onto him and grab his toy.

The child grabbed from may resist, physically or verbally;

may chase and grab back; may cry; may look to an adult for help; or he may just give in and relinquish his toy. Thus, Two-and-a-half-year-old types of fights over materials do not as yet take place, as one or the other gives in too easily and too impersonally. A boy may defend his toy from a boy and then give it to a girl. The balance is very delicate as to who gives in to whom. In another six months, children will be more evenly matched as to aggressiveness, and a fight will be more likely to take place.

Many of these seemingly aggressive approaches are not actually aggressive. It is just that children want what they want and, if necessary, hit, push, struggle to get it.

For all this snatching and grabbing, and all the seeming ignoring, Two-year-olds do enjoy the company of other children. But they do it in their own slow, quiet way. That they *are* somewhat interested in each other is shown by the rudimentary imitation that often occurs. One child may put a ball on the end of his stick in playing with a pegboard, and others follow suit. Or one child may wash his doll in a washbasin, and then others do the same.

It is interesting to note that children at Two are highly individual and somewhat unpredictable with regard to what they may do in any given play period, or in the extent to which they interact with other children.

Any grouping, or lack of grouping, changes so rapidly that the whole situation in any room full of half a dozen Two-year-olds changes almost constantly. Any one child may contact half a dozen areas of interest in as many minutes or may, conversely, just stay in a single place. But few stick with anything, or anybody, more than a short time.

One child may join another at clay play or in "bathing" dolls in a tub of water, may pause momentarily to "paint," may pound on a pegboard, may whirl around or jump up and down, may pause to look at a pet guinea pig or rabbit. One child may cling to his mother (if she is present). Another may ignore any or all adults. One may eagerly watch some other child or children; another may ignore all other children present. One may be very grabby and disruptive of what others are doing; another may make no trouble for anybody.

One's best bet, as an adult, in planning for or supervising any group of Twos, may be to provide a reasonable number of toys or areas of interest (especially to provide some large, undemanding focus such as a sandbox or table for clay around which children may group) but to keep an absolutely open mind—or hand—as to what they may do with toys or materials or other children. Be ready to calm down any small disagreements or problems that may arise. And then just wait and see what happens.

Parents should not be discouraged if the sociality of children of this age does not seem to amount to much. It can be disappointing, after you have gone to the trouble of getting children together, when they often do not seem to pay very much attention to each other. We assure you, getting them together *is* worthwhile.

How and where to get them together becomes the choice of the parent. Outdoors may be the preferred place. That is why we need more nearby small play areas, within easy walking distance of home, where young children can be together. The equipment need not be elaborate. A good-size sandbox is imperative. Swinging is the Two-year-old's favorite activity. Chair swings would make him feel safest. How he delights in swinging next to another child! Low climbing equipment is also much enjoyed.

A good nursery school, if such is available, and especially if it is set up so that mothers can stay when needed, will of course provide suitable equipment and suitable opportunity for play, both indoors and out.

THE TWO-AND-A-HALF-YEAR-OLD

With the Two-and-a-half-year-old, things are considerably different. Many now are, some of the time at least, rather beyond mere parallel play, and there is often considerable interaction. But this interaction cannot in most instances be described as *cooperative*. In fact, it is often quite the opposite.

In associations with other children, at this age, one rule seems cardinal in the child's mind. This is that he is going to hang onto and defend to the death any toy he has played with, is playing with, or might play with. His possessions are almost a part of himself, and to give up anything is highly painful to him. "Mine!" is still a key word to him.

Things are much more important than people, and his own wish to do anything to please others is minimal. To his way of thinking, he himself is the one to be pleased. The Two-and-a-half-year-old has relatively little interest in his contemporaries, though admittedly more than he had six months earlier.

But aggressiveness and the need to protect and dominate any toys or play materials tend to get in the way of any cooperation. Children grab, command, refuse, hit. In fact, the dominant drive at this age tends to be the effort to try, either verbally or physically, to keep others away from their things. They are all too quick to strike out at others, for the most part over property rights.

The child wants everything to come to him. He says "Me," "Mine," "I need." But obtaining objects from others is no longer easy, since the child grabbed from may now resist vigorously, both physically and verbally.

Life is also complicated by the fact that the child of this age finds it extremely difficult to take turns. His attention span and his waiting span are a little bit better than they were at Eighteen months, but not all *that* much better.

This tends to be an aggressive age, and play with children as well as with objects can be quite violent. Both verbal and physical aggression are conspicuous. Some is for the purpose of protecting possessions. Some seems quite unprovoked. There may be much hitting, slapping, pushing, screaming. Or a child may walk up and push another child over and then knock his (block) house down. Children may bump into each other intentionally. Materials may be torn or broken in the course of a dispute. Many children are still more aggressive spontaneously than responsively. Some may not fight back even when toys are snatched. Children at this age are seldom able to resolve their own altercations, so that without adult supervision, group play may very quickly deteriorate.

Relations still tend to be tentative and experimental. Even aggressions are often experimental, as if the child wonders what kind of response he will get. Thus, a child may hit, grab at, or push another child and then look closely to see what is going to happen.

Since children themselves have so little ability to adapt to the demands of others, much help from an adult will usually be needed. It will help considerably, when John demands the tricycle that Jerry is playing with, to say to John, *"When he's finished,* you can have it," or to say to Jerry, "It will be *his turn* pretty soon." Or, if the equipment in question is not too cumbersome or expensive, to have more than one of whatever it is.

Knowing all this, a parent, baby-sitter, or nursery school teacher will pattern her guidance accordingly. She will try not to think of the child as "good" or "bad," as "generous" or "ungenerous," as "cooperative" or "uncooperative." Rather, she will set up those situations, or give those directions, that will help him use his extremely immature and un-practiced social abilities most effectively.

A seesaw *does* take two to play. Clay play, obviously with plenty of clay for everyone, or side-by-side painting with separate easels and sets of paints can encourage rudimentary social behavior.

Parallel play is still conspicuous. Though now there is somewhat more cooperative play than earlier, self-initiated relations predominate since the child is still extremely self-centered. But, during periods of calm, when possession of some object is not in question, there may be seen the bare beginnings of cooperative and/or imaginative play. Children seem very unskilled at this and may regard each other tentatively and seem to be fumbling for a relationship and

24

a way of playing together. Any two may regard each other and may engage in the beginnings of friendly conversation. "Who's ready for dinner? How about some ice cream?" one may say. (Imaginary dinner, imaginary ice cream.) Or, a child may call attention to his own (imaginary) activity: "See, I made a birthday cake."

Cooperation may succeed at the simple level of chasing each other and laughing, but anything much more complicated is likely to fail. Even if one child starts a simple, friendly conversation, the other may very likely not respond. The most frequent interchild exchange, as noted, is quarreling over possessions. However, even those who play alone do tend to watch other children much more than they did just a little earlier.

The tendency to drift toward an adult or toward some type of interesting play materials, seen earlier, continues. As children move on toward Two-and-a-half, interesting materials alone may draw them into a group even without an adult being there to add interest, though adults still seem more appealing to many than do other children. A boy may approach a girl who is showing her doll to a grown-up, even though he ignored both girl and doll when they were alone.

However, for all the quarreling, the parallel play, and the beginnings of cooperation, it is not at all unusual for an entire group of Two-and-a-half-year-olds to be engaged in solitary play, with little if any attention to each other.

SIBLINGS

Perhaps the most important "other children" any child will associate with, at least if he is a member of a more-than-one-child family, are his own siblings.

Most children of Two or even of Two-and-a-half do not have vast difficulty with siblings, and, if they do, as a rule they are more on the receiving than the giving end of the difficulty. Except in a rather crowded family, the Two-year-old is likely to be the youngest of the lot. Older brothers and sisters either quite naturally treat him reasonably well, since he is the "baby," or at least are admonished by their parents that they *must* treat him well. Older sibs are told not to hit him, not to grab his toys, and to let him play with them. If trouble ensues in spite of these admonitions, parents are, as a rule, quick to protect his rights.

With younger siblings, if any, Twos vary. Some are extremely protective, thoughtful, friendly, and even tender with their baby sib. Others, if insecure themselves or if people make too much fuss over the new baby, may be extremely hostile, jealous, and even attacking. Sometimes rough treatment of the baby occurs simply because Two does not appreciate his own strength and the relative

fragility of the infant. Sometimes it occurs intentionally because he really wishes to do harm.

If your Two-year-old seems likely to harm his baby sister or brother, a lot of talk to the effect that "We must treat Baby nicely," will probably not suffice. The two children will need to be watched or separated. A Two-year-old could, only partly unintentionally, do considerable harm to an unwatched baby.

So, don't leave Baby alone with him, even though he may seem kindly.

chapter four

TECHNIQUES

"Techniques" is another word for little tricks that, often used almost automatically, can help your Two-year-old through his sometimes difficult days. Behavior-modification people tell us that we can get almost anybody to do almost anything we want him to by praising the good and ignoring the bad.

This may be true in general, but with the very young child a little more is needed. Young children are, perhaps fortunately, very vulnerable to the many tricks and techniques that many mothers and fathers use almost instinctively. Not every single problem of the day has to be worked out at a rational level. A good technique can be worth its weight in gold. Here are a few that have been found to work.

First of all, *take advantage of the child's ritualistic tendencies*. Do this by setting up rituals of your own to get him through the rough spots of the day. A good bedtime ritual, for instance, especially at Two-and-a-half, may solve that often very difficult problem of getting the child to bed.

Such a ritual may include first undressing, then the bath, then pajamas being put on and teeth being brushed, then a swing on a doorway swing, then going to the bathroom, then bed and a certain number of certain bedtime stories, then a hug and goodnight kiss, and then lights out.

All of this may seem to take rather a long time, particularly if you yourself are tired. But by following some such routine you are more likely to end up with your child in bed and asleep than if you just attacked the bedtime hit-or-miss or head-on.

In fact, *the more you hurry, the longer time it may take.* If you are impatient and try to speed things up, your child will sense this and will drag his feet even more than usual. It is best not to try to shorten your routine or to skip any part of it. Just throw yourself into it. And if you are interrupted, as by the phone (but protect yourself from this if possible), don't try to pick up where you left off. Reconcile yourself to the fact that you may need to go back to the beginning and start all over again (skipping the bath, of course). Only as your child approaches Three will you find that you can chip away at the edges of your total bedtime routine.

Thus, it is wise in setting up routines that are going to be practical for you to follow day after day not to include too many items in an excess of goodwill and friendliness. Once an item has been included, it will be very difficult to get it out.

With a child of this age, it is important that you *accept his need for sameness.* Two likes sameness. He likes repetition. So far as is practical, permit his toys and other possessions to stay where he puts them, furniture in the household to remain where he expects it to be. He wants everything in its proper place; not only in what he considers its proper place but also at its proper time, each activity of the day following in its customary and predictable order. He likes to know how things will be.

Accept and even welcome the *security measures* your child sets up for himself, such as his favorite toy or blanket or even his own thumb. They may be lifesavers if you find it necessary to travel or to move. In strange surroundings even a small bit of security can mean a lot. And even in everyday surroundings there will be frequent and strong needs for his bit of security.

Even as earlier, take care of the child's lack of inhibition (it is still hard for him not to grab at forbidden objects) by what we label *household engineering*. Put your most valuable or most breakable objects where he cannot reach them. Or, by means of gates or other barriers, keep him out of the more fragile parts of your house. This does not amount to a lack of discipline. It is not giving in on your part. It is common sense. When he is a little older and his own inhibitors are a little stronger, "discipline" will be easier and more effective.

Give *face-saving commands* as much as possible. Try not to trap yourself in some inflexible demand such as "You have to pick up *all* your toys before you can have dinner." Far better to suggest, "Let's pick up the toys now." Then, if he absolutely refuses to take part in the pickup, you will not be stuck with trying to push through an order in which you may have lost all interest before the situation has terminated.

Good face-saving techniques include:

Say, "Let's do so-and-so," and then, if need be, you can do the major part of the work yourself.

"How about doing so and so?" is also good. If his answer is "No," so be it. You can give up on the whole thing without embarrassment.

"We'll go out to play just as soon as we have picked up." Again, going out to play is the behavior stressed, and if you have to do most of the picking up yourself, your failure to get his compliance is not too conspicuous.

"Where do the blocks go?"—when it is pickup time— may motivate the child to put them where they belong. If he doesn't, no matter.

A good face-saving technique, *after* a child may have refused, is to make a joke or some humorous remark. Or, change the subject or leave the scene completely.

If you have a clinger, you'll find that a confident manner and a direct statement of intention will get you much further than a hesitant request. So, if you wish to leave your child, as at nursery school or a play group, don't *ask* him. *Tell* him. Don't ask, "Is it OK if I leave now?" Rather, tell him, "I'm going to the store now, and I'll be right back."

For best results, *bypass the rigidities* of Two-and-a-half whenever you can. Try to avoid head-on clashes as to whether he will or will not do what you want him to. Chances are that he will not, and if you insist on meeting resistance head-on, *you* are apt to be the loser. Instead, divert him when you can from what is going on.

If, for example, your child doesn't like to get dressed, try to avoid big arguments about whether he will or will not allow you to put his clothes on him. Instead, set him up on some rather high place and dress him quickly, all the while talking rapidly about some future happening.

In fact, it is often possible to *divert* a child of this age with conversation. A good deal of talk tends to confuse the Eighteen-monther, but a rapid patter, even though he may not entirely understand what you are saying, often serves to fascinate and calm the Two-and-a-half-year-old. And at least it may distract him from whatever position he has taken that is making difficulty.

Avoid the dangerous word "later." Try to avoid giving the child of this age a peg on which to hang his opposition. If, for instance, he wants to do something that will not be appropriate until later, avoid that special word. It will merely activate his own "Now," and you may find yourself engaged in a tiresome and fruitless game of "Later," "No, now," "Later," "No, now." Instead, if it must be later, say something like "OK, we'll do that, but first let's do this or that." You elaborate cheerfully and positively until (hopefully) he has entirely forgotten his original demand. Or at least you may have stalled him along until actually it *is* later.

If a request cannot be granted, *distraction of any kind* may be your best bet and is highly preferable to fighting things out with his own weapons. So, distract; or, even better, *terminate by changing the scene*. If you find your-

32

self involved in one of those fruitless (and boring) "I want—I don't want" routines, in which the child demands some toy, food, article of clothing, or activity, and then the minute he gets it rejects it, and then when you take it away wants it again, it may be impossible to resolve the situation at his level.

You will need to break into his impasse. This is best done by shifting to entirely different ground. You can do this by leaving the scene, taking *him* away from the scene, or introducing some entirely new object or idea.

For instance, when the child is in a bad mood and nothing pleases—he doesn't want to stay, but he doesn't want to go (and this, of course, is often the case when he isn't in a bad mood)—some simple suggestion such as "But where are your shoes?" can shift his attention, with good results. Also, don't give him more than one or two chances to make up his mind. If it becomes clear, and it often will, that he is not going to be satisfied with either of two alternatives, just pick him up and remove him from the scene, or otherwise terminate the situation. He may cry and scream, but this is preferable to continuing on and on with a fruitless, frustrating, and rather ridiculous, "Do you want to go home now?" "No." "Do you want to stay?" "No." If nothing pleases, so be it!

Distracting and terminating may be two of your very best techniques when your child is Two-and-a-half. *His* best technique is to trap you in his own frustrated back and-forthness. Whatever the situation, the child of this age tends to want the *opposite extreme* of whatever you want him to do, or even of what he himself has chosen. You have to help him break into his own back-and-forth-ness. You almost have to explode him out of his rigidity. This can, of course, be done by your bursting into tears and saying, "You don't love Mommy." It can be done by spanking him or shouting at him. Far better just to distract and change the subject or the scene, if you can.

Since choices are so very hard at this age, it sometimes helps if you can *program the child* by telling him in advance just exactly what is going to happen. Thus, you say, "We are going to the store. You are going to ask the man for chocolate cookies. He is going to put them in the bag for *you* to carry. Then we're coming home. You may eat one on the way, and you will save the rest."

His repetition of this sequence of events will show that he at least understands what you are saying and *may* carry it through. But, even with such careful planning, chances are that you may have left out some important detail, and chaos may still descend. (If you can allow this excursion to be just for him and not part of your own shopping, it can be a potentially happier and more successful experience).

Most conducive to the more relaxed atmosphere that the child of this age needs but cannot produce for himself is the soothing presence of *music*, in almost any form. Mother's singing can help. Chanting a request on a minor third, as "Time to come to breakfast," may be more effective than a direct command. Records, especially nursery rhymes, are just the thing for those low periods at the end of the morning or afternoon when tantrums are so frequent. Some children, especially boys, like to have their own phonograph and may play their own records for very long periods of time.

And what about *those terrible tantrums*? Most parents find that their best bet, once a tantrum has begun, is to ignore it as much as they reasonably can. A young child's tantrum can become a powerful weapon *if* he finds that his parents will do almost anything he wants once he throws a tantrum. So, as difficult as it may be for you, it is very important that the child find out as soon as possible that his tantrums are not going to gain him anything, even attention.

But of course your very best technique as far as tantrums are concerned is to prevent them before they begin, if you possibly can. Most parents know what times of day or what kinds of situations are more than their youngster can stand. At least half the trick, where tantrums are concerned, is to keep your child out of the kinds of situations that are going to be just too much for him.

Giving *chances* is a technique that works very well with some children at some ages. Even Two-and-a-half may be too young, with some, for this technique. You can try it, and you'll find out very quickly whether or not your child is ready for it. For some, if they do something very badly or if they refuse outright to carry out some command or suggestion, saying, "Well, I guess you're going to need three chances on that. Let's try again," works very well. That is, you give the impression that an initial failure or refusal is not noteworthy or harmful and that people quite naturally expect a person to make more than one try.

Questions, if adroitly asked, make excellent motivators for both the Two- and the Two-and-a-half-year-old. As a question, "Where does your coat go?" is apt to gain a much more positive response than the command "Hang up your coat." However, be sure to avoid questions that can be answered by "No," such as "Do you want to go in now?" And, even at Two-and-a-half, any verbal techniques may still need to be supported by action. In fact, often sheer action alone (such as leading the child to the bathroom if you think he needs to use the toilet) works better than even the cleverest verbal technique.

One of the potentially most useful, and at the same time potentially most dangerous, of all techniques at this age is the giving of *choices*. Parents often ask us, "Do you believe in choices?" Well, we do and we don't. The whole area typifies the paradoxical character of preschoolness. Used wisely, the giving of choices can get you through many a tense moment, through many a difficult day. Used unwisely, they compound your difficulties.

Your very best and chief use of choices at this age comes in situations where the child is stuck and can't move forward, but in which his compliance, at least his compliance in some certain way, is not essential. That is, giving choices can be an excellent motivator if it really doesn't matter too much which alternative is chosen.

Frequently you can end dawdling and delay, can get your child out of his stuck patterns, by giving some simple choice, such as, "All right now, do you want the blue one or the red one?" Or, "Shall we wash your hands before or after we listen to your record?" Or, "Do you want me to read the book about shoes or the book about Billy?"

(Especially at Two-and-a-half, the child will usually choose the second alternative simply because it was mentioned last. So, if you yourself do have a preference, it's wise to mention your preferred choice last.)

The feeling that he himself is making the choice, that he is doing what *he* wants rather than what *you* want, that he really has the situation right in his own hands, can at times be so marvelously effective that parents sometimes fall into the trap of over-using choices and of using them in certain situations, or with certain children, where they will not be effective and may actually be obstructive.

And it can indeed be a trap since there are many situations in which, and many children for whom, using choices can be the worst thing possible. For example, if your child is over-tired, it is unlikely that he will be able to make a good choice or that he will be happy with any choice he may make. When children are tired it is important to simplify the situation, not to complicate it by allowing them to make their own choices.

Nor is it wise to give choices in really important situations where it seems necessary to you that the child act in a certain way.

But perhaps the most unfortunate time for the giving of choices is when you and your child are involved in some new or difficult situation. If, for instance, you are eating out, don't complicate matters by giving him too much of a choice as to what he will eat.

Above all, don't rely on the simple trick of giving a choice to solve for you complex problems that only time, great skill, and considerable insight will eventually solve. "Choices" are not magic. They can do only so much.

Also, personalities differ with regard to choices. There are many children of such a clear-cut temperament that they know their own mind and find it easy to make a choice and to stick to it. These children enjoy the sense of freedom and self-expression that being allowed to make a choice can give. With such boys and girls, giving choices is almost a sure-fire method of gaining ready and enthusiastic cooperation.

However, there are children who by temperament seem almost constitutionally unable to make a choice. For instance, there are the confused children who do not seem to have any idea of what they want. If you give them a choice, you merely confuse them more.

Similarly, there are the vague children who by nature seem to have very little structure to their behavior, and who need to have structure provided by the environment. For such children, giving choices only increases vagueness. What they need is a clear-cut pattern or direction they can follow. They want and need to be told *exactly* what to do. One mother had an ironclad rule that no exceptions to basic procedure were to be allowed at dinner, even when guests were present.

There is another type of child with whom the use of choices doesn't work very well. This is the kind of child with whom *no* techniques seem to work. If you give them any possible loophole, such children will start vacillating. If they are given any leeway at all, a simple trip to Grandmother's can be complicated by questions of whether they will or will not go; what they will wear; whether they will sit in the front seat or the back seat of the car; who will sit beside them; and so on and on. For such children, the only effective approach is to tell them specifically and rigidly just exactly what is going to be done, and to insist that your orders be carried out.

(Many parents find that having their preschooler always sit in the back seat of the car prevents exploration of the dashboard and interference with the driver. If the car seat is placed in the back seat, on the side opposite to the driver's seat, then the parent can more easily see what the child is doing and can talk to him more easily.)

So, with a child who needs rigidity, when preparing for a trip to Grandmother's you state: "We are going to Grandmother's. You will wear your red snowsuit. You will sit in the back seat of the car. When we get there, you will get right out of the car and go into the house." If there is any difficulty along the way, it is wise to pull over to the side, stop the car, and wait until the child is ready to carry out your directives.

And, lastly, there is the just naturally oppositional child who almost automatically opposes whatever anybody suggests, or even what he may *think* anybody else wants. Dealing with him is too complicated a matter to be solved by so simple a solution as merely giving choices. Trial-and-error can tell you, if your own prejudgment does not, whether or not yours is a child with whom you can effectively use this potentially very helpful technique.

THINGS TO AVOID

We have found that if you will try to follow some of the suggestions we list here, it can be tremendously helpful in getting along with your Two-year-old.

1. Avoid any expectation that all daily routines will go smoothly. Even if *you* do your best, your child will not always cooperate fully.

2. Do not introduce any sudden changes in routine without warning or without some cushioning buildup.

3. Avoid any questions that can be answered by "No," such as, "Do you want to have your bath now?"

4. Do not give choices when it matters.

5. Do not expect your child to wait for things or to take turns easily.

6. Avoid ultimatums, such as, "You have to eat all your lunch before you can go out and play."

7. Avoid getting all upset by your child's demands and

rigidities. Try to see these behaviors not as badness or rebellion but rather as immaturity. Try to appreciate the wonder and complexity of growing behavior, even when it makes trouble for you.

8. Do not be surprised or upset at "No" or "No, I won't."

9. Do not take away or object to your child's security blanket or favorite, bedraggled toy. Do not fuss at him when he sucks his thumb.

10. Do not expect your child to share easily with other children.

11. Do not be surprised if you are unduly fatigued at the end of the day.

12. Even if your boy or girl behaves exactly in the manner we describe in this book, avoid merely sitting back and telling yourself that he is just "going through a stage." He will be going through a stage, but that doesn't mean that you simply wait for the next stage. You treat him, discipline him, help him, punish him if you must, in your own best way. It is just that knowing that certain undesirable behaviors may *be* just stages gives you reassurance that other children, too, behave like this, that even bad behaviors can be "normal," and that this, too, will pass.

13. Don't start teaching any Two-year-old to read. Read to him—do—but don't feel that you must start teaching him *anything*, at least not in a formal way.

14. Don't worry about your child's IQ (intelligence quotient). There's nothing we know of that you can do that will actually give him a "superior mind" if the genes you have handed on did not already arrange for that.

15. Refuse to get mixed up in your child's "Mommy do," "Daddy do" routine, which may be so strong at Two-and-a-half. If it is perfectly convenient, allow the person he prefers to take over. But if substitution is not convenient, *you* keep on helping, whether he prefers you or not.

16. Don't get your feelings hurt if *you* try to help your child and he wants somebody else. This is just his contrary way and does not mean that he doesn't like you.

chapter five
ACCOMPLISHMENTS
AND ABILITIES

THE TWO-YEAR-OLD

Children vary tremendously in their accomplishments. There are the early talkers who by Two years of age already have a tremendous vocabulary. There are others, equally intelligent, who, especially if they are boys, may not have much to say until they are Three or older.

Interest in books and in formal learning also varies tremendously. It is extremely important not to compare your child's intellectual or academic accomplishments with those of others, since each child has very much his own timetable.

It is also important not to feel that you as a parent "ought" to be doing something *special* about your child's intellectual life. As Dr. Arnold Gesell wisely remarked, so long ago, "Mind manifests itself." The child's mind is not something separate from the rest of him. Rather, he demonstrates to us the state of his mind by almost everything he does. He walks, he runs, he climbs, he looks, he listens. He grabs a toy from another child. He refuses to have his coat put on. Or, he models clay, messes with his fingerpaints, builds with his blocks.

All these things that he does are examples of his mind in action. It is not necessary for him to learn letters and numbers—now, or even when he is Three or Four—to show

you and others that his mind is in good working order. If he does show such interest, play the game—any game that suits his fancy—as he acquires a mastery of both letters and numbers. But remember, as with the growth of any behavior, interest may come and go. At any rate, try not to be self-conscious about your child's so-called *cognitive development*. This is just a term, vastly overused, that has come into the literature in recent years.

If your boy or girl has good potential, and if you provide a reasonably rich and lively environment and give him plenty of love and attention, his mind will take care of itself.

Remember, always, that each child matures at his own rate. But here are a few of the things the ordinary Two- and Two-and-a-half-year-old may be able to do that it may interest you to know about.

MOTOR BEHAVIOR

The average Two-year-old has his body in much better control than he did just earlier. He is now much surer of himself than he was, and his body in action gives him fewer surprises. His abilities have increased to the point where he can run without falling, walk up and down the stairs alone (even though he still uses two feet to a step), walk on tiptoe, march in time to music, jump off a low step.

However, motor behavior, whether of arms or legs or total body or merely of fingers, is still broadly undifferentiated. Thus,[1] Two's gait is constrained because of lack of freedom at both ankle and knee, so that he walks with an up-and-down tread. Foot and leg move as one rather than as articulated parts whose different motions will later be integrated into a smooth walking pattern.

The child still has difficulty in using one hand independently of the other. If he holds out an injured finger for bandaging, he tends also to hold out his matching, uninjured finger as well. His fingers tend to work all together as he scoops up small objects. He is likely to curl

all his fingers as you try to straighten them out in order to put on his mittens. And there is as yet, in many, little differentiation of handedness. Even a child who may eventually turn out to be fully right-handed may now use his left hand almost as much as his right.

The Two-year-old is rapidly losing the physical proportions of babyhood. No longer does a disproportionately large head make him look so topheavy. And his gait is no longer a baby stagger or toddle, though it is still short-stepped and constrained compared with what will be the freedom of his Three-year-old walk. The same lack of freedom in ankle motion that influences his walking is also seen as he propels a Kiddie Kar. He moves his car by pressing down with his heels and pulling forward, while his foot rocks down to a toe-to-floor position as the car moves along.

Another characteristic of the Two-year-old in motion is that he tends to use both arms and legs in pairs. It will be well on toward Three before he can easily alternate either. But oh, what speed the adept Two-year-old can master as he propels Kiddie Kar or other wheeled object.

Another kind of lack of differentiation is seen in that the child of Two does not separate his goal from his way of achieving that goal. Activity is typically undirected, unaccented, unphrased. He climbs the Jungle Gym as much because he likes to climb as because he wants to get to the upper level. He fills his pail with sand not so much to have a pailful of sand as because he likes putting sand into his pail.

However, in spite of this immaturity, behavior does show a little more direction and a little less randomness than it did even six months ago. Now in seven clocked minutes of play in a nursery playroom, we see the child covering much less ground than he did just earlier. Instead of seeming to think almost entirely with his feet, he now sights an objective, visits it, even though briefly, sights another, visits *that* briefly, and so on. But powers of concentration, admittedly, are still so limited that he pauses only briefly at any one spot of interest, then, as a rule, moves quickly on toward another. (*See* Figure 2.)

Fine motor behavior, too, is becoming increasingly skillful. Children can now put together simple puzzles—with rather large pieces—and like to work with paintbrushes

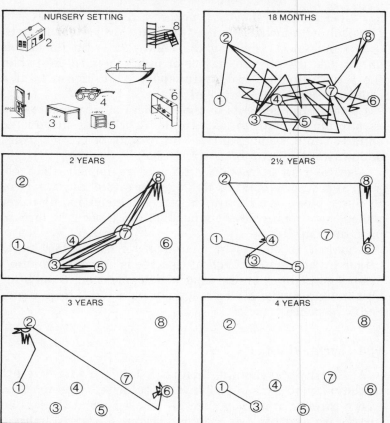

Figure 2
Seven Clocked Minutes of Nursery School
Behavior at Different Ages

and crayons, even though movements still often involve the whole arm. They can turn the pages of a book singly. Two can make a fist and then wiggle his thumb, or move each finger separately. Some enjoy finger-play games.

They enjoy toys that have big pieces that can be taken apart and put back together again. They love to string large beads on a shoelace, unscrew the lids of jars, cut Play-Doh with a cookie cutter, turn on (low) water faucets.

But in almost anything the child does with his hands at this age, the process may be of much more interest than the actual product, and, fortunately, self-criticism is at a rather low level at this still early stage.

Certain arrangements of the physical environment serve as unfailing stimuli to activity. Steps or rungs inspire the child to climb, inclines invite him to walk or creep upward or downward, apertures are irresistible.

Also, objects in motion attract more quickly than objects at rest. The child of this age loves to chase a ball, or to totter along after a wagon. (At Eighteen months they pulled; now many love to push. They especially love to push their stroller.)

And just as objects in motion prove irresistible, so do people in motion. The child of this age is an adept imitator, even of something as fine as a facial expression, though his best imitation, like his best activity, is a total gross motor bodily response.

VISUAL BEHAVIOR[2]

At Twenty-one months there is a tendency for one eye or the other to turn out of line on occasion. This tends to worry parents, who may then be relieved when their child turns Two and his eye behavior becomes more stabilized. An occasional turn is no longer seen unless the Two-year-old voluntarily crosses his eyes inward—an act that is usually quite upsetting to his grandparents.

An eye examination will, as a rule, show nothing to be wrong. However, any *persistent* turning of either eye should be checked immediately with a competent vision specialist who is accustomed to working with children. Such advice as "He'll grow out of it" should be looked on with suspicion, and another diagnosis should be sought. Persistent turning *is* serious, and there is no reason to assume that he *will* grow out of it.

The typical Two-year-old shows increasing visual interest in objects at great distances. He may even spot a "car like Daddy's" a block away. He is becoming a good observer. His vision is now more sensitive in the marginal areas, and so he is distracted easily. With his increasing visual range, he likes to move and to explore.

Not all of Two's visual activities are active and impulsive or related to distant objects. He may entertain himself by thumbing through the pages of a picture book. Recognition of pictures is an early form of reading. Working with clay or Play-Doh, he looks closely at what he makes. But seeing an object is not enough as Two depends strongly on manual manipulation of any object in order to understand it better.

As he reaches Two-and-a-half, the child's visual behavior may seem increasingly rigid. Transitions in vision, as in other areas, may be hard for him to accomplish. If he looks away from an object that interests him, he may have difficulty finding it again with his eyes. For this reason, it helps him to have manual contact with his toys.

He is becoming aware of opposites in many things. In his social world, he is trying to understand such things as "you and I," "yes and no," "come and go," "fast and slow," "person and object." His eyes and his intelligence cannot yet tell him what is right and what is wrong, so to deal with such problems he is often ritualistic in his behavior. He wants things kept in order—right where they are. In his space world the opposites he deals with, and sometimes has trouble with, are near and far space.

Moving objects away from him helps guide his eyes into outward space. His eyes take the lead in seeing objects; thus, he may move toward them to make contact. At the same time, movements of large objects (such as a truck) coming toward him may produce screams of terror. He may accept them better if he can hold his mother's hand.

The Two-year-old is beginning to understand the use of the word *where*. He can respond with his eyes to explanations of where things are. Yet he may be unaware of the

47

space between where he is and where the object is—a dangerous situation if the ball he spies has just rolled across the street. In action he may tend to lose his marginal areas of vision and miss things outside his direct line of vision, such as cars coming toward him as he chases his ball.

His advancing use of eyes and hands together brings a wider group of toys into his domain. He enjoys blocks for building, jars with screw tops, simple wooden puzzles of two or three pieces, interlocking toys, and pounding toys. Increased use of eyes to guide hands makes fingerpainting, clay work, crayoning, and sandbox play useful and enjoyable activities for exercising his newly found eye-hand coordination.

As the child nears Three years of age, an interest in objects at great distances should normally be coming in. Parents should consider the need for professional eye help if their child seems unduly restricted in his visual interests and seldom or never gives attention to things at a distance. Unawareness of activities and movement to one side may be associated with a developing amblyopia (lazy eye). Careful parental observations of how the child sees may be the first step in detecting and eventually correcting visual difficulties. Professional help should always be sought if you are worried about anything connected with your child's visual behavior.

ADAPTIVE AND PLAY BEHAVIOR

Two has all the world to learn, and so he touches everything—not only touches, but tastes as well. Whatever attracts him, or actually almost anything that comes his way, he explores tactually. Most contacts are brief, whether with objects or with people.

Since his attention span is very short, his threshold of distractibility low, and his inhibitory apparatus only slightly developed, almost anything can attract him, but few things hold either interest or attention. A fleeting contact, and he is off to something else unless held in place by an especially interesting object or by adult intervention.

He enjoys almost anything that comes his way, though his use of toys and materials, his attention to books and pictures, is not lasting. He may enjoy the activity of painting, though his product will have little structure. In fact, in painting as in other situations, it seems to be the action (making large, messy strokes with his brush) rather than the end product that is of interest. Fingerpaints may be more fun for him than regular paints since they provide livelier action with more feel to it. He loves modeling clay, though here again his products do not amount to much from the adult point of view.

On specific request, the child of Two can imitate both a vertical and a circular stroke but is still a long way from making either letters or numbers. He can, if asked, build a tower of six or seven small blocks.

He likes to fill his pail or dish with sand and stones, dumping and throwing. Any water play, if permitted, will be a highly favored activity. He also likes to play with blocks (especially large, colored blocks) in a gross motor way. Here, as in painting, the product is not so much fun for most as the activity. What most children like best about blocks is not the thing they build as much as manipulating them, piling them together, filling wagons with them, dumping and lugging them around.

Boys and girls of this age often show not only great interest in but great love for their very own books. They like to look at simple books with good, clear, uncluttered colored pictures with few details. The very best book for a Two-year-old is written in simple language, has not too many words to a page, and is highly repetitive in both words and ideas. The size and shape of the book is also important. Twos love little, tiny books, or books of an interesting shape like *The Tall Mother Goose*.

Two likes to be read to if the story is not too long or complicated. In the interests of brevity, you may wish to skip certain parts of the story. (This is not practical at Two-and-a-half and Three, when the child may require that the entire story be read, over and over, word for word.)

His favorite story topics are things he does himself, moments and activities of his own day, or stories about his very favorite object—his shoes. (He will be especially captivated if you substitute *his* name for the name of the child

in the book.) He may like to talk to or about the people or animals in the illustrations. He likes to listen to nursery rhymes and then to repeat them to the adult.

Most enjoy music, singing phrases of songs, though not on pitch. Most also enjoy any rhythmical equipment, such as rocking boats, swings, or rocking chairs. Almost all like watching a phonograph operate as they listen to records. Some can operate their own phonograph.

Both boys and girls now like to play house with dolls and stuffed animals. As a rule there is not much structure to this kind of play. The Two-year-old directs the greater portion of his doll play to covering his dolls with covers, painfully picked out one by one and spread as smoothly as his skill allows, over face and body alike. Sometimes brief admonitions to "go to sleep" accompany the covering.

Bedding tends to be the favorite activity in doll play, but domestic play also includes having dolls or animals be sick, asleep, cold, warm, or nice. The child may "read" to his baby, may change him, give medicine, take him for a ride, feed him.

Some domestic play does not include dolls. The children act out their own eating or sleeping. Then bedding play means the child's lying down and covering himself with some piece of material. Eating means scooping imaginary food into the mouth or drinking imaginary liquid. Going for a ride or visiting may involve trains or boats or airplanes made of blocks or boards. Dressing up at this age goes not much farther than putting on a grown-up's hat.

As Louise Woodcock points out in *Life and Ways of the Two-Year-Old*, the basic reality to the Two-year-old is himself. (Or, his own possessions, especially his shoes.) So, in his free dramatic play he likes to live over and over again all the intimacies of his personal life—being put to bed, going to the toilet, eating, having his hair cut, being given medicine. His own daily life is the area of his keenest, most active interest. He makes himself the point of reference in most of his observations. When somebody else bumps a finger, he reassures himself, "I didn't bump *my* finger." When he sees another eating, he may remark that his own toast or cracker is "aw gone."

Out for a walk, the child not only is interested in his own process of locomotion but also loves to touch things he sees along the way. He likes to pick up sticks and stones, or leaves. He loves to walk on curbs and on top of low walls. He dawdles and dallies and is in no particular hurry. In fact, as in so many of his activities, he enjoys what he is doing for its own sake rather than for any purpose (or destination) involved. If you can manage to slow your pace down to his, both you and he should enjoy your walks together. If you are in a rush to get where you are going, your impatience will interfere with his enjoyment.

Birthday Parties. One important aspect of the child's play life, which, perhaps fortunately, turns up only once a year, is his birthday and its attendant birthday party. Though some parents do manage not to celebrate a child's first birthday lavishly, not too many can hold out beyond that. So, a party for the second birthday is a customary part of family living. Even this can be quite successful if parents can manage to restrain themselves.

A Two-year-old may even know the meaning of the word "party." But this is no reason for the elaborate planning and execution of a party for a gathering of sometimes as many as twenty people, when four or five might have been a better number.

A party for a Two-year-old is best planned with his social immaturity clearly in mind. His concept of a "party" is perhaps related to a tea party, which he may have imitated in his daily play. Thus, the sheer manipulation of dishes and the pouring of some kind of liquid may make the party a party for him. Guests may not be an important, necessary, or even expected adjunct.

However, most Twos are beginning to know the word "present," so they will enjoy receiving presents and tearing the paper off their gifts.

As to guests, one grandmother or other relative added to the family group may be quite enough. The immediate family will be more able than outsiders to conduct the party at the child's level—opening the presents, pouring the milk, eating the food provided. And they can permit this all to go on at the child's own pace.

It might be better not to have other children, except for his own brothers and sisters, at this gathering. If other children are to be present, they should be few in number and should be invited to stay for only a rather short time, ideally just long enough to consume the refreshments, give their gifts, and perhaps each to receive a small present in return.

LANGUAGE AND THOUGHT

Those unacquainted with the preschool world might feel that the ordinary Two-year-old does not have enough language for us to say much about. Not so. Most are now well beyond the jargon stage, and many talk in sentences of three words or even more. Vocabulary shows a sharp increase and may include as many as two or three hundred words. Though parts of speech mean little yet, the Two-year-old has discarded jargon, speaks in phrases or in three-word sentences, uses prepositions or verbs substantively, may use pronouns correctly, and may employ a single word to cover a variety of experiences.

"Mommy" may be his word for any adult female. (But, although one Two-year-old girl named all five females in a room as "Mommy," she called four by the expression "A Mommy" and then gleefully pointed to her own mother as "The Mommy.")

Twos may still refer to themselves as "me" or merely by

their proper name. For most, it will be another six to twelve months before the important word "I" comes in. But his own name means a great deal to the child of this age. His active need to build up his own identity and sense of self is seen in his effort to strengthen the bond between himself and the name that was given him. Children of this age can become quite upset if called by a name other than their own, though later on this same mistake may be considered fun and funny.

Most have not yet clearly distinguished things from people and so may freely confuse animate and inanimate. Sometimes a child may talk to clothes and toys, to trees plants, and doors, or even try to climb into a truck he sees in a picture book. A favorite ritual at this age is to say "goodnight" to all the objects dear to him, preparatory to going to bed. It is a lovely game to play: "Goodnight clock, goodnight chair, goodnight door, goodnight doorknob, goodnight stairs," and, finally, "Goodnight, Mommy."

However, for all that his language may still be limited, it now has many uses. Even when alone, the child may use *verbal sound effects* to accompany solitary play: "Brring," "whang-whang," "Zoom-zoom-zoom." Or he may chant or sing as he runs around the room. He may even give himself verbal directions: "Jump," "Rock," "Go up dis way." In fact, many Two-year-olds talk to themselves quite as much as they do to other people.

Talking is still used to a great extent as a running accompaniment to action or even as a play activity in itself. But now it is also being used extensively as a means of communicating not only wants and needs but also ideas and information.

Twos very much enjoy combining motor and verbal and vocal activity. When the child manipulates small objects with his hands, he often carries on a running commentary. When he rides his tricycle or pulls his wagon, he often accompanies this activity with crooning or chanting.

Words and their combination into sentences come in so gradually that the adult is often unaware of how much effort is involved. Sentences increase in length in almost simple arithmetic progression. First the child combines two words, then three, then four or five. One by one, missing articles, prepositions, and auxiliaries come in. But grammar remains shaky. Thus, the child may say, "Her come to see we. Us not visit she." When a new word comes in, he often uses it excessively until it becomes a familiar part of his vocabulary.

Only a few question words are present at two years of age, but an important new word that has come in is "yes." "Why?" may come in as his own response to a direct request before it comes in as part of his own question about the why of things.

The child begins now to think of an agent behind an action, as "The car is broken. Jimmy broke it." Or, he may say, "The rain has stopped. Who stopped it?"

If you are so minded, and feel that your child needs any special stimulation so far as his use of language is concerned, at two years of age, and increasingly thereafter, you can stimulate his use of adjectives through giving him experience with different sounds, textures, colors and sizes. Listen with him and comment about loud sounds and soft, big things and small, soft things and hard. It is not good to make a real "lesson" of such conversations, but they can be fitted nicely into daily play.

Or, if you wish to make your reading to the child an opportunity for stimulating language, you can ask him: "Show me the boy," "What is the girl doing?" Or, you can talk about colors or shapes or sizes. Much that most parents teach their preschoolers comes about quite naturally as you talk to them, read to them, take them on walks. It is natural for any parent to wish to share his or her knowledge of the world with the child.

However, as Laurie and Joseph Braga[3] correctly point out,

> Although this period of time in the children's development is marked particularly by their growth in language

development, and that in turn affects their thinking skills, it should be remembered that children still know most of what they know through means other than words. For example, children who learn to apply the words "rough" and "smooth" to objects do not learn about those qualities through learning the words. First they must perceive the qualities.

This is one of the many reasons why we warn parents about strenuous early efforts to teach young children to read. It is essential that they have many experiences of the world about them before they try to read about these experiences. Otherwise, the words they read will have little meaning.

LANGUAGE AND OTHERS

If a Two-year-old is in a social situation with both adults and children, he is more likely to talk to the grown-ups than to the children. Figure 3, which reports our own long-term observations, shows that the typical Two-year-old talks mostly to himself, second most to any familiar adult present, little if any to another child or other children. And most of his talk tends to be self-initiated rather than in response to something said to him. In fact, there is a good likelihood that he may not reply even if *you* speak to him. *He* is the one who decides whether there will or will not be conversation. Typical of the Two-year-old conversationalist is the child who says to her mother, "Look, Mommy, leaf," and then to any other adult who may be present, "I show Mommy leaf." (In fact, you may find that, if you approach a quiet Two-year-old in a somewhat rough-house way, he may respond better than when approached too directly with words. His body does not seem as vulnerable as his mind or personality, and the physical approach may seem less threatening or invading to him than words addressed directly to him.)

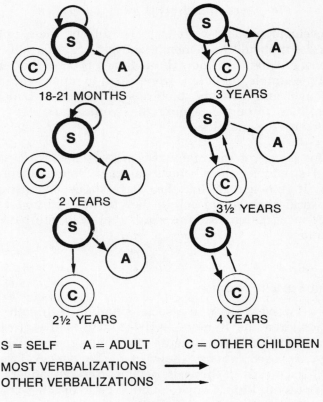

18-21 MONTHS

3 YEARS

2 YEARS

3½ YEARS

2½ YEARS

4 YEARS

S = SELF   A = ADULT   C = OTHER CHILDREN

MOST VERBALIZATIONS ⟶

OTHER VERBALIZATIONS ⟶

Figure 3
Person to Whom the Child Talks Most

The child now has many different ways of approaching the adult with words. Single-word sentences are now replaced by two-word phrases or even three-word sentences. The child makes simple statements about objects present, about members of his family, about things he does or does not want to do: "Here's a car-car," "More juice," "Thath cute," "Here's a baw," "Too many people," "Me climb," "Where Doan?," "Daddy gone."

He now likes to show and name objects, seeming to experience more fully through naming: "telephone," "choo-choo train."

Requests for help may still involve merely looking at an available adult or pulling him or her by the hand, or they may now involve two or three words: "Wanna get down," "Wanna see fish."

The child may ask for the name or location of an object: "What's this?" (or, "What's dis?") or, "Where baw?"

Most give information now in short phrases instead of in single words as earlier: "All dirty," "All clean," "All finished." They like to be appreciated: "Watch me," "Lookit my shoes."

Some verbalization consists merely of social greetings: "Hi." Some involves direct commands: "Read book," "Put back." Or, a highly imaginative child may explain his own imaginary play "Cookin' eggs."

In response to an adult's comment, the child may merely imitate what is said to him instead of responding. Thus, he may repeat, "What's Baby doin'?," or, "Go find Kafr'n." He may or may not respond to verbal commands, such as when asked to fetch an object. In fact, he is still most influenced by the physical approach (picking him up and putting him where you want him to go).

However, the Two-year-old may answer a simple question and may engage in very simple conversations. Thus, if told that the snow is coming down, a child may ask, "Why?"

There is *still relatively little conversation with other children*, and what there is, is mostly self-initiated. The largest amount of verbalization tends to be directed toward protecting his own property: "No," "Don't touch," "That's mine." Or, the child demands an object being played with by another: "That's mine," "I want cup." He may say, "Look out," reinforcing his command with a push. A girl may complain, if another child pulls her hair, "Hurts." About as far as most go socially is to say "Hi" or "Hello."

Nobody has to tell you how your own child expresses *refusal*. He does it by crying, screaming, tantruming, by saying the actual word "No," by slamming or stamping out of the room—all depending on the circumstances, his exact age, and his own personality.

It might interest you, however, to know a little something about the way the more or less typical child of Two says "No" to situations he is not willing to accept.[4]

His main way of refusing at this age is not verbal but *motor*. The typical Two-year-old, when he does not wish to comply with an adult request, typically gets up and down from his chair, leaves the examining table entirely, explores the room, runs around the room, or hands things to his mother instead of playing with them himself.

However, not all refusals are motor. Some refuse by speaking (or not speaking) or respond by showing emotion. Thus, when a Two-year-old does not wish to comply with an adult request, his outstanding verbal response is a simple "No." Or, he refuses to respond at all. Or, with a simple one- or two-word sentence, he requests some other activity.

Emotional refusals consist of clinging or referring to Mother, refusing to play with or respond to the materials presented, or refusing even to sit down at the table when toys and materials are presented.

Figure 4 demonstrates that at Two years of age the outstanding kind of refusal to comply is motor. By Two-and-a-half years, verbal refusals already occur equally as often as do sheer motor refusals.

TWO-AND-A-HALF YEARS

MOTOR BEHAVIOR

Coordination is now much improved over what it was six months ago. Now the child can walk on tiptoes, can jump with both feet. He will, if requested, try to stand on one foot. He can climb and slide quite skillfully.

He can also modulate. He can speed up, slow down, dodge obstacles, turn corners, make sudden stops, and then start up again. He can step over low obstacles. At some time during this year most become able to throw a ball with some accuracy, kick a ball with ease, and catch a large ball with arms and body.

Fine motor behavior improves too. The fingers are now more differentiated from the hand as a whole, and the hands are less likely to open and close as a unit. His fingers do not all close up as you try to get a child's mittens on.

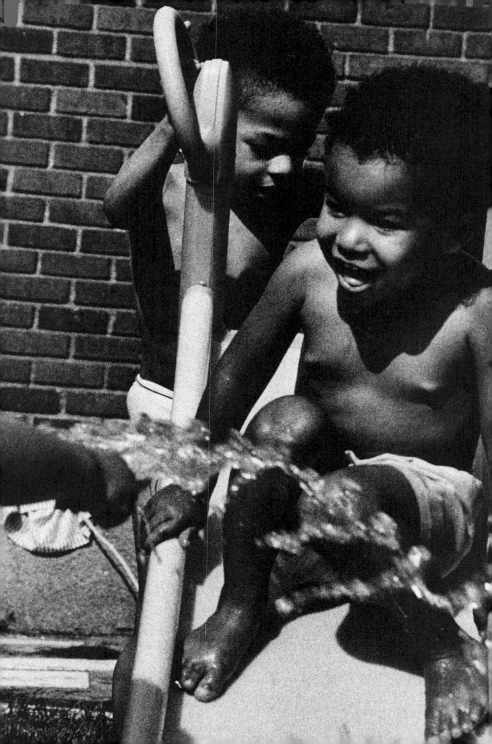

Also, as hand differentiation develops during the year, there is less and less of the earlier simultaneous action of both hands. And as the child comes to the more directed use of tools, he is more and more able to use only one hand to do his work.

The child now does all the things he did six months ago but does them even more skillfully. Bead stringing is more effective—fewer beads are spilled. Painting, though still not very expert as far as product is concerned, shows a little more effectiveness of wrist motion and a little less whole arm stroke. The child does better with puzzles, is even more skillful in manipulating small toys or parts of toys.

In many, handedness is not yet clearly determined. At first the child may shift any tools from one hand to the other. Which hand he uses to hold his spoon may be determined by the side of his plate it is lying on, and, regardless of which hand he starts with, he may shift it from hand to hand repeatedly during the meal. By Three, many have established handedness.

ADAPTIVE AND PLAY BEHAVIOR

If by adaptive behavior we mean problem solving, even the Two-and-a-half-year-old cannot be called particularly adaptive. His perception and comprehension are immature, and thus he has meager tools with which adaptively to solve any problem situation. He will, for instance, make valiant attempts to close a door blocked at its base by a stick or stone, without ever looking downward to discover what it is that is getting in his way. Or, in trying to fit pieces into a puzzle, he is more likely to try to make pieces fit by pounding them *hard* than by turning them.

On the other hand, in a very simple problem situation such as is presented by the three-hole formboard with round, square, and triangular holes and a block to fit every hole, he can place the blocks correctly in their holes without hesitation. And if the formboard is then rotated so that the blocks are *not* below their proper holes, he can adapt with no more than initial error to this rotation.

Many new abilities, not seen earlier, come in at Two-and-a-half. A boy or girl can now imitate vertical and horizontal strokes and can make two strokes if asked to make a cross, even though the strokes may not cross. He can build a tower of eight small blocks. He can repeat two digits.

His *play behavior*, though much like that seen at Two, is becoming increasingly versatile. He now loves to hear stories and enjoys rhythm and repetition in both rhymes and stories. He likes to hear the same story exactly as written, with nothing left out. You will not get far if you try to skip a page or paragraph while reading to him. Though he cannot read for himself, he seems to know his stories word for word.

The child of Two-and-a-half, like the child of Two, likes books that tell of things he commonly sees and activities he himself engages in in the course of his day. He likes to hear stories about getting up, getting dressed, eating breakfast, taking a walk, playing with his wagon, going to bed. He also likes books that give very simple information about animals and transportation, such as *Ask Mr. Bear, A Saturday Walk, The Little Family,* and *The Little Auto.* He now likes to hear the same story over and over again, always in exactly the same way and with nothing changed or omitted. In fact, he begins to know what is coming next and may even like to supply words or sentence endings. There is little demand for plot.

There is at this age a special delight in role playing, in acting out behaviors seen in the adult: feeding a doll, talking on the phone, or even sweeping the floor. The child also loves to fingerpaint, and this remains a better medium than actual paint. Clay, too, is an excellent medium for the child of this age. He can roll it endlessly, forming his clay into snakelike lengths that he can then make into many other forms.

Most very much enjoy play with mud and water, if per-

mitted, making pies and cakes. And sand is always a favorite because it pours so well. Most also enjoy block play.
They especially like building with large building blocks,
which they frequently knock down and climb on.

• *Accomplishments and Abilities* •

Children now like to play with things that can be taken apart and put back together again, such as stacking toys, puzzle blocks, or cars or trains that can be taken apart and then recombined. They also show a strong fondness for their own special toys, particularly their stuffed animals or dolls. (Without any parental pressure, most girls do prefer dolls; and most boys, stuffed animals.) A child may have a large family of these and may like to have them lined up in their own special order. They may also like and need to hang onto their own personal security blanket.

All enjoy short excursions in their own neighborhood. A brief walk right near home is appreciated more by most children of this age than some more elaborate excursions that an ambitious parent might plan.

At this age, as at Two, many children do watch quite a bit of television. It can be an interesting, though not necessary, and usually minor, part of their lives at this time. As a rule, it presents no special problem since even as late as Two-and-a-half, parents can still pretty well control any viewing, determining both time of watching and programs seen. Parents are well advised, instead of merely complaining about the poor quality of programs available, to be careful about what and when their children watch.

LANGUAGE BEHAVIOR

The boy or girl of this age can now give his or her full name if asked, and can name simple pictures in a book. The child may refer to himself as "me," instead of using his proper name as earlier. Thus, he will say, "Me do it myself." Children with early language may already be calling themselves "I."

If a Two-and-a-half-year-old is in a social situation with an adult and another child or other children, most of his conversation is still directed toward the adult (*see* Figure 3, page 58). But he talks to other children more than he did just earlier, and he talks to himself somewhat less.

However, verbalization still accompanies solitary play.

The child may comment on his own activity: "Now go up," "Put some in these holes." He may elaborate on his own imaginary play with talk about what he is doing: "Choo-choo-choo here comes the caboose. For Chicago."

Most of his conversation, if there is an adult present, is directed toward that adult—parent, adult friend, nursery school teacher. Talk is now much more elaborate and versatile than it was six months ago. Vocabulary has expanded by leaps and bounds, and ways of using it are admirably varied.

Thus the child can, in short sentences, announce current, completed, or intended activity: "Me fix it," "Me make it go," "Me made a house," or, "I want to climb." He will ask for help or demand not to be helped (possibly both at the same time): "I need to get down. Help me," or, "Don't push it. Don't help me."

He loves to boast and brag about his own independent ability or his own product or prowess: "I can take my own coat off," "Here I am, way up here, see? I just got up by my own self." Or, similarly, the child likes to tell about being a big boy or girl, or about playing an imaginary role: "I want the big bike. I'm a big girl now," or, "I'm gonna be a store man."

He requests or gives information freely: "Where's that carriage?," or, "I have beads at my house." He is also very free with direct commands to the adult: "Hey, get out of my way," "You move," "Get some for me, too." There are often many complaints about other children: "She's got my toy," "He pushed me down," "He's a bad boy."

Though the Two-year-old is likely to respond if addressed directly by any adult, he is for the most part more interested in what he says to her than in what she says to him. Not only may he not respond verbally when spoken to, but he may not do whatever it is the adult has asked him to do. Many are less docile and less responsive to adult commands than earlier or later. The child may resist or may simply ignore what is said to him.

In a formal behavior-examination situation, as described

in *The First Five Years of Life*, by Gesell et al., the Two-and-a-half-year-old who does not wish to comply has many different ways of refusing. Big gains have been made in the past six months in this respect. Now language refusals are just slightly in the lead (*see* Figure 4), though at this age, for the last time, motor ways of refusing are still prominent.

So, the Two-and-a-half-year-old, if he doesn't want to do what the adult requests, may get up from his chair, may leave the examining table entirely, may climb on his chair, move furniture, or stand to perform.

Language refusals consist mostly of saying "No," refusing entirely to say anything, suggesting material other than that offered, or referring verbally to his mother. Emotional refusals are slightly fewer than at Two, and definitely fewer than motor or verbal refusals.

Now, in play, an increasing amount of talk is directed to other children, though most are still more interested in what they say to others than in what others say to them. Statements of ownership or commands to leave property alone, arguments over property or efforts to secure things from others, predominate: "Get off. This is my place," "You can't have my dolly," "Don't touch," "I want that. That's mine." (Or, less maturely: "Me want dat. Dat's mine.")

Direct commands are given in a domineering effort to control the activity of others: "Ann, get off. Use this," "Get outta here, Bill." Name calling (alas) is prominent: "You bad boy"; as are aggressive threats: "I'll hit you if you don't watch out," "I'll kill you dead."

Some of the more mature can now make polite requests of some other child: "Want to play with these blocks?," "Let me help you," "My need one of these. Sank you." And, verbalization may accompany the beginnings of cooperative play: "We'll make a bed for the baby over there," "Come on for dinner. Who's ready for dinner? All set? No, you sit right there." Or, cooperative exchange may consist merely of conversation: "How you?," "Fine."

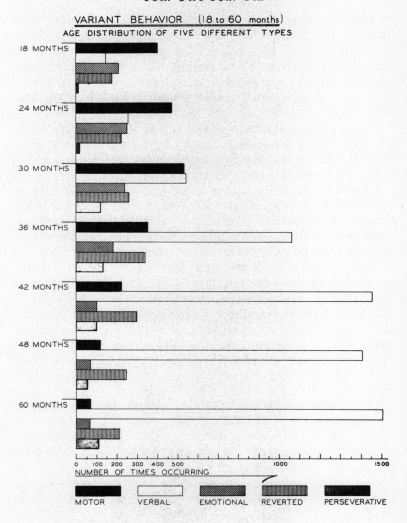

Figure 4
Age Distribution of Different Kinds of Variant
Behavior, from Eighteen Months to Five Years

70

Some like to talk to others about their own activities, real or imaginary: "See, Joannie. I make a birthday cake," "I make a birdie."

Response to the verbal approaches of others remains minimal, though the child may say "Hi" when so greeted; he may say "Not ready" when asked if he is ready; he may say "Mine" when some other child claims ownership of some desirable object. Real back-and-forth conversation is still limited.

chapter six
HELP WITH ROUTINES

In his daily life, and especially during his daily routines, the child is beginning to be extremely repetitive in both speech and action, increasingly so as he moves on toward the exacting age of Two-and-a-half. This demand for sameness and familiarity and for having things *just so* can make routines extremely difficult for any caretaker. For a while around Two, things may not be too difficult. But by Two-and-a-half, one treads on very thin ice, since compliance can very quickly turn to firm objection.

EATING

The child of Two can feed himself to some extent. That is, he can inhibit turning the spoon so that an increasingly large proportion of food gets into his mouth. He can hold his cup or glass in one hand, with the free hand poised, ready to help if need be. He can lift, drink from, and set down his glass or cup skillfully. By Two-and-a-half, he can even use a fork effectively.

Appetite tends to be rather good now, and mealtimes should go along reasonably well if mothers are knowledgeable and wise and do not fall into any of the usual traps.

To begin with, one should not expect three "good" meals a day. Be satisfied with one hearty meal—most usually

supper—and get what food you can into your child at the other meals.

Accept the fact that refusals and preferences tend to be *very* definite at Two and even more so at Two-and-a-half. Respect these preferences. It may be color that determines your child's preference—he may prefer red and yellow foods and dislike green. Or, his sense of form may make him prefer whole things—whole beans, big pieces of potato—unless he demands the exact opposite, the continuation of pureed foods.

There are some at this age who are eager to try new foods; others who insist on the true and the tried. Some like their foods mixed all together. Others like them so separate that they do not even want two different kinds of food to touch on their plates. Some like their food cut up into very small pieces; others want everything whole.

And, most children of this age are extremely determined about the kinds of food they will and will not eat. In fact, this is a high point for food jags and demands for repetition of favored foods. It is just as well to adapt to that eternal dessert of apricots night after night, or that everlasting spaghetti. Food jags run themselves out more quickly if you accept rather than combat them.

It is important not to force either type or quantity of food. Your child, if healthy, will probably have a good appetite and should be a good eater if you don't spoil things by needlessly insisting that meals go *your* way.

Since very young children love between-meal snacks, set a certain time for these and provide nourishing foods, such as fruits and carrot sticks. You do not want your child to be snacking all day long, but there is nothing wrong about a planned between-meat bit of nourishment.

Even when nothing else is accepted, most will eat crispy, circus-type foods, such as popcorn, peanuts, or crackers.

Most children can feed themselves at least part of their meal by now but may require help as they tire. Some will feed themselves the foods they like; will allow Mother to feed foods they are lukewarm about; absolutely refuse other foods no matter how they are offered. Most can manage both spoon and cup, though there will still be some spilling. This bothers only the extremely neat, who, after spilling, may demand that Mother take over the feeding process.

If your child's sometimes poor appetite bothers you, you

might try keeping a chart of the food eaten. You will probably find that good days balance poor days and that he is not really starving himself to death.

Since there tends to be a great liking for sweets at this age, candy had best be kept out of sight and out of reach, or even out of the house. If you wish, homemade candy without artificial coloring or flavoring can be provided occasionally as a special treat.

As a rule, the more casual and confident you are about mealtimes, the better things will go. In the (unfortunately quite natural) battle for supremacy between parent and child, children are very quick to spot areas in which parents are vulnerable. If you can force yourself to remain quite calm as to whether or not, or how much, or what, your child eats, chances are he will quickly appreciate that this is not an area where he can cause excitement or get satisfaction by objecting and insisting.

One can practically guarantee that a normally healthy child will not starve himself to death.

BATH AND DRESSING

The bath is still a favorite activity for many and is enjoyed thoroughly by most. By Two, the child is becoming increasingly interested in helping wash himself. He especially likes to wash and dry his hands, though he is not too skillful at this. By Two-and-a-half, he is even more eager to take over the bath routine, and his characteristic rigidity may result in his insisting on things being just so. He may love to slide back and forth in the water, and might go on endlessly if not prevented.

Or, he may build up his own special ritual involving shining the fixtures with his washcloth or putting in and/or taking out the plug in a certain way. He may lose all sense of the bath as a place where he is washed, and may insist on his special routines.

Getting the child out of the tub may be difficult, and is quite dependent on the ingenuity of the parents. The re-

moval of the plug, with the subsequent running out of the water, makes some children fearful that they, too, may go down the drain. Therefore they hop out at once. Others are not in the least fearful and continue to slide back and forth even after the water is all gone. Then tricks of getting them out, such as counting, will need to be used.

Whatever the ritual he sets up, the child's special demands in relation to his bath may be tiring and time-consuming, but, so far as you can, if you give in and do things *his* way, this routine will go more smoothly.

As for dressing, the Two-year-old is better at undressing than at dressing. He can take off his shoes, socks, and pants. He may try to put some of his clothes on, may be able to pull on a single garment, but is usually not too successful. He *will* cooperate as *you* dress him (at least while he is still Two), but on his own dressing abilities tend to be limited to putting on socks and sometimes shirt, pants, or coat.

At Two-and-a-half, most are still better at undressing than at dressing, and, in fact, may take clothes, especially shoes, off often during the day. Dressing abilities continue to be limited to putting on socks and sometimes dress, shirt, pants, or coat. If the child does try to dress himself, clothes are apt to be put on backward, heels of socks may be over the instep, both feet may be in one pants leg, shirts may be on backward, shoes may be on the wrong feet.

Two, whatever his abilities or inabilities, is usually not very demanding about the whole performance. But by Two-and-a-half, dressing can provide an especially prickly problem. With his characteristic rigidity, the Two-and-a-half-year-old may insist on dressing himself entirely (even though he cannot really do this), or he may insist on some definite order of dressing, or he may insist on or refuse certain articles of clothing.

He may accept such necessary help as having you place his shirt on the floor with the back uppermost, or his pants ready to slip into. Even if he will not permit you to touch him, he may accept suggestions. Or, he may, of course, go to the opposite extreme of demanding to be dressed entirely by you. Then, having demanded help, he may complicate matters by going limp, like a doll or a baby.

Temper tantrums over dressing are not unusual. The child may not only insist on or refuse special articles of clothing but may also try to escape. He may even run away or hide under the bed where it is hard to reach him, and may become violent if caught and picked up. (If he has just been bathed, and is wet and slippery as well as elusive, dressing may indeed become a difficult chore.)

You may need to close or even lock doors to keep him within reach. If you put him on a high hamper from which he cannot get down, it may help to streamline your efforts at dressing. If you do this, try to avoid an argument as to whether he will *stay* on the hamper or not. Instead, talk about some interesting future event. But even with your best efforts the child may alternate between demands for complete independence and insistence that you do everything for him. He may also get into an argument as to whether or not he will get dressed at all. He may refuse to cooperate even in the simplest ways, such as thrusting his arm into an armhole.

Speed on the part of the mother and a refusal to allow herself to be drawn into arguments about what he will or will not do, or how he will do it, are useful.

Though dressing ability is still limited at Two, the child of this age takes great pride in his clothes—his hat, his handkerchief. He especially loves his *shoes*. "New shoes" may indeed be one of his favorite phrases, and he can often be approached successfully by the stranger who comments on his shoes.

Like his six-months-earlier self, the Two-and-a-half-year-old also loves his clothes. He is especially fond of hat and mittens. He may at this age definitely prefer clothes he is used to over new ones and may cling to any old clothes just as he clings to any of his other possessions. It may be a task to get him to accept anything new. For some, familiar clothes seem to be almost a part of the self and are not dislodged easily. In fact, many in a strange place cling to all their clothes and may refuse to remove even their outer garment.

BEDTIME

With the very young child, bedtime is perhaps the very easiest routine. Young babies often fall asleep the minute they are put into their cribs, or even fall asleep while nursing, before they are put down.

But around Two years of age, if not before, trouble begins. The Two-year-old boy or girl, often gentle during the day, may be very difficult to manage at bedtime. Though he may go to bed willingly, after that, trouble begins. He may remain in bed but call out with his many demands— a drink of water, another hug, to go to the bathroom.

It is often difficult, especially with a first child, to know just when the demands represent real needs (the child may really need to go to the bathroom) and when they are merely stalling tactics.

Even more troublesome than the called-out demands are those which the child makes in person. If he can get out of his crib, he often appears and reappears in the living room. Though a certain relative permissiveness *may* work best with some aspects of the day's routines, here firmness tends to pay off. After a reasonable response to what seem the more pressing demands, the time does come when Mother or Father will have to make it clear that *this is all*. Mother may be able to handle this herself, but Father's firm voice[5] may need to be raised to stop these seemingly endless demands.

One thing you *can* do, in an effort to simplify bedtime for a Two-year-old, is to anticipate as many of the child's demands as possible. Be certain that he *has* been to the toilet, has had his drink of water, is provided with his handkerchief and with whatever bedtime toys he likes to take to bed with him. If yours is a child who is afraid of the dark, leaving his door ajar and leaving a light on in the hall, or providing one of those little pictures that glow in the dark, may solve the problem. Give him his goodnight kiss. In fact, a short snuggle time with him to begin with may prevent tiring demands later on.

By Two-and-a-half, demands come earlier, before the child gets into bed. In fact, getting him into bed at all may be quite a fight. And bedtime can be complicated by very strong demands for pre-bedtime activities. With his love of sameness, the child of this age may set up quite an elaborate bedtime ritual, one that will have to be carried out in full detail *every night*, before he will get into bed. These rituals can be the despair of an entire household, and they tend to get built up before the adult fully realizes what is going on.

So, there may be the saying-goodnight ritual. The child may have to say goodnight to, or kiss goodnight, every person in the household, in just some certain way and in some certain order. A certain number of kisses. The exact same words to be said to and by everyone.

Then there can be a going-upstairs ritual; a getting-undressed, being-bathed, having-teeth-brushed ritual. And everything in just the exact same way and in just the exact same order. If the ritual is interrupted, it often cannot be picked up where it left off but may need to be started all over again.

And then the pre-bedtime play! If on one occasion you have rashly read three stories, played two phonograph records, allowed a little athletic activity, this may be demanded every night.

Rituals *can* be a help in getting the difficult and determined child of this age into bed. But if he realizes in advance what he may be getting into, the prudent parent will try not to let too much of a ritual develop in the first place.

Some extremely rigid children may need to arrange all their belongings in just some certain order, every night before they get into bed. And some are extremely rigid about what they take to bed with them. For many, a favorite snuggle toy will suffice. With others, demands are more exotic. We knew of one little boy who required, every night, a hammer, a green pepper and a very sharp pencil.

Will the time ever come when your boy or girl will not need these rituals any longer? Indeed it will. Usually sometime around Three years of age they become much less important, much less necessary. They do not as a rule drop out all at once, as one might wish. But you can tell when they are losing their grip if, when you cautiously omit one tiresome item, it is not noticed and demanded.

Probably the majority of Two- and Two-and-a-half-year-olds are reasonably good sleepers. A few seem to wake at the slightest sound and demand attention.

Or, the child may be bothered by dreams. With most, a small amount of friendly attention induces a return to sleep.

Demands to sleep in the parents' bed are best handled according to the individuality of the child. If you have a child of an extremely flexible temperament, an occasional giving in to this request will probably do no harm. But if your child is rigid and inflexible, just giving in once may set up a more or less permanent demand and is best not tried.

All advice about bedtime may be easier given than carried out. Perhaps the majority of children are reasonably good sleepers. But with his insatiable demands a difficult child can produce almost unbelievable family upheaval (Mother's wish to keep him happy and quiet; Father's insistence that whatever it is has gone on long enough).

At both Two and Two-and-a-half, perhaps the majority of children go to bed between 7:00 and 8:00 P.M. and sleep around eleven hours a night. (If you are lucky.) However, most tend to wake rather early. If you are fortunate, your child will entertain himself until he is ready to get up. It is a good idea to provide him with books or toys that, hopefully, will hold his interest until your own time of waking. For some reason, putting the child to bed later at night in the hope that he will sleep later in the morning does not seem to work very well with most. Some, perversely, if put to bed later than usual, seem to wake earlier than usual.

Nap. The nap can be the high point of the day for many mothers. It not only provides the child with much-needed rest and relaxation, but it gives Mother a breathing spell and a few precious moments to herself.

Two-year-olds, like younger children, still tend to be rather good nappers and may even sleep for two hours or more. Two-and-a-half-year-olds tend to have more trouble with naps. They can now climb out of their cribs, and this may have to be accepted. (It really doesn't matter, especially, if you provide a comfortable place on the floor, whether they sleep in their beds or elsewhere.)

Tying their door loosely will at least keep them in their room, and from now on a "play nap" may have to be accepted. Even a play nap serves its purpose.

If the child does sleep, he may be very cranky on waking. Best to approach him obliquely, perhaps moving around the room somewhat noisily but not approaching him directly until he has time to come fully awake.

Most children wake of their own accord after an hour or two. If they sleep much longer than two hours, this late nap tends to displace night sleep, so as a rule it may be best to terminate it yourself, if need be.

ELIMINATION

As the child moves on into his third year, many parents become a little more serious about efforts at toilet training. Most Twos are not yet able to stay dry, even during the daytime, though many can "tell" when they need to go to the toilet. Also, dryness after the nap may well have come in, presaging longer periods of dryness at other times of the day. Bowel functioning is often under control now. And, as the year goes on, more and more are able to stay dry.

In fact, many parents find that if they can hold off *vigorous* efforts to get their child to stay dry, sometime around Two or Two-and-a-half most children can and do stay mostly dry during the daytime, largely of their own accord. Even in a nonpushy family, the child knows what is expected of him, and most are pleased to stay dry as soon as they are able. (Many mothers do find that, around two years of age if they provide a set of little steps to be placed in front of the adult toilet, this helps and encourages the child to go to the toilet by himself.)

Our culture has relaxed a great deal about toilet training in the past twenty years or so, and most young parents themselves tend to be quite relaxed about it. The end result is that children probably become dry at about the same time as always, or perhaps just a little later, but there is a great deal less fuss about the whole procedure than there used to be.

Dryness at night is highly variable. Those children who do remain dry may actually sleep right through the night, or may call two or three times during the night, asking for toileting. The majority need to be picked up, or are picked up, and may still be wet in the morning. Opinion differs as to whether children should be thoroughly waked when they are picked up for this, but most parents find that it disturbs the child less if he is *not* waked up.

If the child is already wet by nine or ten o'clock, chances are that he will not make it dry through the night, even with pickups, so some parents feel it is not worth the bother. Rubber pants and cloth or paper diapers are still in order for most, whether they are picked up or not, to restrict dampness.

Bowel accidents are rare as late as Two years of age. Things go best if Mother is not too insistent on daily performance, since some children quite normally skip a day now and then.

When bowel accidents persist, it tends to be more in boys than in girls and may be one way these children have of controlling their mother's actions. For those who are not really having accidents, but are simply not trained, we recommend the "newspaper-on-the-bathroom-floor" approach. Allow the child to run around in the bathroom with his pants off at about the time when you expect him to function, and tell him that he can use the newspaper on the floor when he is ready. (If he has not yet settled down to some particular time of day, he is not ready for even this simple approach.) Best have the newspaper in a corner of the room as this seems to make the child feel more comfortable. Once he has trained himself to the newspaper, you can introduce a potty chair to the scene, and then gradually move him from the potty chair on the floor to the regular toilet.

Stool smearing, if it persists this late, may occur at the end of the nap. Tightly fastened diapers reduce the likelihood of this unattractive, though basically harmless, behavior.

If adverse emotional factors are not involved—that is, if the child is not persisting with bowel accidents as one aspect of a battle with his mother—training is usually effected in a rather remarkably short time.

Girls, especially, may have a long daytime span of five to even ten hours between urinations, and three or more days may elapse between bowel movements if you don't check up. Children need to be helped not to put things off too long. Play with water, a favorite pastime, may help them to urinate. And being read to as they are seated on the toilet may produce the needed relaxed atmosphere for them to release their bowel movement. Laxative fruit juices or specific laxatives prescribed by your pediatrician may occasionally be needed.

chapter seven

THE MENTAL LIFE OF THE TWO-YEAR-OLD, OR HOW HE SEES THE WORLD

Adults wonder a great deal as to what the young child thinks about. "I often wonder what goes on in his little head," parents say.

Fortunately, we don't have to let it go at wondering, for the young child has many ways of telling us what does go on in his little head. Words are his clearest way of telling us, and by Two, or at least Two-and-a-half, most have enough words to convey a reasonable idea of what it is that they *are* thinking about.

But we don't have to wait for Two, and we really don't have to wait for words. As Dr. Arnold Gesell so often repeated, "Mind manifests itself." And mind does manifest itself in almost everything the infant or young child does. If your baby, lying on the floor, sees a ball out of reach, gets to hands and knees, creeps toward the ball, picks it up, and brings it to his mouth, all these actions are expressions of his mind at work. He doesn't have to tell us in words that he sees and wants the ball and is determined to get it. He shows us, by his actions, that this is the case.

In recent years parents have heard a great deal about *cognition*, about the child's *cognitive sense*, about his *mind*. One would almost think the mind had just been discovered. And some authorities tell you that it is important for you

to cultivate that mind, to develop it, to do something special about it.

Certainly you will want to be responsive to your child's activities and interests. Certainly you will want to provide books and toys and music and pictures. Certainly you will talk to him and play with him and take him for walks and do what you can to enrich his surroundings.

But we guarantee that you don't have to do anything special or academic about your child's mind or his intelligence. If he is born with a reasonable amount of native intelligence, and if you surround him with a reasonable number of toys and books and things to look at and play with, and if you provide a reasonable amount of time in which you and he or she can enjoy each other, his mind will take care of itself.

But just because it is not really all up to you, as some quaintly put it, "to give your child a superior mind" does not mean that you won't be excited about his developing awareness and ability. And because words do remain your very best clues as to how his mind is developing, you may be interested in knowing something about the way in which some of the young child's more customary concepts normally develop.

So, here are some of the things we have observed in Two-year-olds in relation to their sense of time, sense of space, sense of number, sense of humor (rudimentary as it may still be in some), and verbal creativity.

SENSE OF TIME

This may seem like a rather abstract concept. It may not seem too necessary for a parent to know all about his or her Two-year-old's sense of time. And yet even this can be useful in your actual daily handling of your boy or girl.

The Eighteen-monther lives in the immediate present. He wants what he wants *now*, and "later" is not a word that means very much to him. The Two-year-old also lives rather much in the immediate present, but even by Two most children can respond positively to such phrases as "in a minute," "soon," "pretty soon," "Pretty soon it will be time to ——."

The Two-year-old still lives chiefly in the present and now understands quite a few different words for that present: "Now," "today," "aw day," "dis day" may well be in his vocabulary. He also has a few words of his own for future events: "gonna," "in a minute." As a rule he has no words for things past, though he is beginning to use the past tense of verbs (inaccurately).

He is also beginning to have a slight concept of sequence. In nursery school, "Have clay after juice" is a meaningful explanation to him of the way things are going to happen.

By Two-and-a-half, he is even more sequence minded. He can express this for himself: "Daddy come home. Then dinner." And he will also respond to another's explanation of what comes after what. And, for most, there is a sudden expansion in the number of different time words used. It is not unusual for a child of this age to have as many as twenty or more different time words of his own.

Also, the past has come in. The child now freely uses words implying past, present, and future and usually has several different words for each. There are fine divisions of time—"morning" and "afternoon" have been added to "day" to indicate present time. The future may be indicated by "someday," "one day," "tomorrow," "pretty soon." Past time is usually generalized to "last night." Even though "tomorrow" is used, the word "yesterday" has not appeared.

Nor does the child differentiate between things just past and those long past. Most, freely even if inaccurately, now use the names of the days of the week, though the concept of *month* is still far beyond them.

SENSE OF SPACE

The child of Two has come a long way past his Eighteen-month-old space vocabulary, which may have consisted solely of "up" or "all gone." Now he uses many different words relating to space.

Though Two is not a particularly expansive age, there is considerable expansion from the earlier "here-and-nowness" as shown in the use of such words as "there," "where," "other side," "outdoors," "upstairs," "up high," "go away," "fall down," "turn around."

The more complex notion of "container" and "contained" comes in with "in" and "out," though even at Two-and-a-half the child may get both legs into one pants leg. The Two-year-old can use space words both spontaneously and in answer to such questions as "Where is Mommy?," "Where is Daddy?," "Where do you sleep?"

Through movement, many are now learning a sense of up-and-down, front-and-back. Many, in a test situation, can obey four directions with a ball. They can put a ball on a chair, on a table, can give it to Mother, and can give it—if requested—to another adult. But for all this versatility, they still are not able to put the ball *under* or *beside* a chair.

Also, the Two-year-old's sense of space is such that he enjoys the challenge of walking on curbs and on (low) walls. Playing near a wall is of interest at Eighteen months; but most are Two before the word "wall" comes in, and Two-and-a-half before they know "corner."

By Two-and-a-half, perhaps predictably, the sense of space becomes more insistent and more exact. The child not only wants things right where he puts them, or right where he thinks they belong, but he can talk about "right here" or "right there."

His space vocabulary has now expanded. In fact, *more new space words are added to the child's vocabulary in the six-month period from Two to Two-and-a-half than in any other six-month period.* (This is in contrast to the most new *time* words, which come in between Two-and-a-half and Three years of age.) The increase in use of two space words combined gives exactness to location: "right home," "way up," "in here," "under the table." This exact use of space words is very much in keeping with the rigid, exact behavior characteristic of this age.

Also by Two-and-a-half, many children are becoming aware of where things in the household, and different people's belongings, "go."

"Near" represents an advance over the earlier "in" or "at." A beginning interest in distance may be expressed by "far" or "far away." The child may even expand to the point of talking about a nearby town or city, as "to New York."

When out for a walk, he does not merely bumble along

happily but randomly, as earlier. Two-and-a-half goes for a walk with a thought of destination. In fact, on a walk or ride he may not only have his destination in mind, but tends to be so extremely space conscious that, as we've said, he may want to take exactly the same route every time he goes out.

By Two-and-a-half, the location of beings other than Mother and Father is within the child's conception. He can give a reasonable response to such questions as "Where do birds live?," "Where do fish live?," "Where do airplanes fly?," "Where is the roof?," "Where is the chimney?" Most can also give some kind of sensible answer when asked where they live, though the actual name of their street does not come in until Three years of age.

Responses to space questions, at first rather general, soon become more specific. At Two years, if asked where they sleep, most will answer, "At home," or, "In my crib." It is not until Three that most will reply, "In my room." Similarly, if asked where Mommy cooks dinner, the Two-year-old is likely to reply, "At home." By Two-and-a-half, he can elaborate with, "On the stove." Or, when asked where he eats dinner, the Two-year-old is likely to say, "At home." By Two-and-a-half, he can add the detail of, "On the table."

NUMBER SENSE

The number sense of the Two-year-old is still very rudimentary. He can, however, distinguish one object as different from more than one. Thus, he can say "Two balls" when handed a second ball. And he can sometimes distinguish two objects as distinct from more than two. As a rule he cannot go beyond this unless given very special training. Most cannot yet count beyond two, if that far.

As to plurals, to begin with, children name a first object "ball," and then any other of its kind is merely referred to as "more ball," or "other ball." When, as is the case with many at Two-and-a-half, they become able to use and understand the word "two," everything more than one may become "two." Most do not get up to three until they become Three years of age.

The Two-and-a-half-year-old, with his rigid sense of just how he wants everything to be, may insist, as when he has a cookie, on having *one for each hand.* He may also be much upset, as again when he has a cookie, if a bite is taken out or a piece broken off, insisting that everything be whole and round and unbroken.

Though many at Two or Two-and-a-half begin to use words like "another," "big," "little," or "much," which help them understand a little about quantity, and help them compare things by amount, they may not yet be able to tell, when asked, which of two things is bigger.

SENSE OF HUMOR

The sense of humor, which most of us consider such an essential ingredient of the human personality, actually develops rather late. Even very tiny babies do smile, but it is probably more in friendliness or in feelings of comfort or pleasure than in amusement.

Even at Two, humor tends to be rather rudimentary, but it *is* expressed. Or at least children *do* smile, mostly at grown-ups. In a situation in which a Two-year-old plays in the same room with an adult and other children, the largest amount of smiling accompanies spontaneous verbal-social approaches to the adult. The child's own gross motor activity is the next leading source of smiles, with friendly smiling at the adult (peek-a-boo or chasing), unaccompanied by words, coming next in frequency.

Actually the situation in which the child smiles most—his verbal approaches to the adult—involves neither real humor nor even much imagination. He merely calls attention to some aspect of his own activity that pleases him.

But there may already be a smattering of humor. The incongruous quite definitely pleases. Thus, the distinction between what goes on one's toes and what goes on one's fingers is still so new that to confuse the two, such as to

say that mittens go on one's toes, seems very funny to most. Or, a child may pretend to put a cracker in his ear instead of into his mouth, and then smile at *this* incongruity. Or, he may pull his jacket off inside out, and that may amuse him.

Though the most joy is felt at the child's own gross motor activity or at his own success, there is some smiling related to other children, even though for the most part this may not be entirely friendly. One child may offer a crayon to another and then playfully snatch it back, or may grab something from another. The height of friendly, smiling play may be a brief game of peek-a-boo.

But even six months more diminishes egocentricity and increases the amount of laughing and smiling at or with some other person. At Two-and-a-half, in a situation with an adult and other children, social approaches and responses to the adult come first as smile producers, while approaches to another child (though usually still without verbalization) are usually physical.

Thus, in verbal-social approaches to an adult, a child may merely call attention to his own activity, to an object that he holds, or to his own prowess or product. Verbal-social approaches to other children may include silly vocalization, chanting, repeating words, explosive speech, teasing. Both the words "fun" and "silly" are used spontaneously. There may be hugs or attacks, either of them accompanied by a smile. Or, a child may merely share an activity, such as rocking, with another child, and smile. Motor activity combined with talk and an aggressive attack on some other child for the first time produces smiles.

Examples of humorous situations at Two-and-a-half follow:

Incongruity. A child stands in his coat cubby, then rides backward on his tricycle, mentioning in a very loud voice that he had *chairs* for breakfast, or he may talk about wearing pajamas outdoors.

Teasing. A child starts to hand a toy to another child and then teasingly snatches it away.

Accident. Falling down, choking, falling over and getting stuck in a chair, falling off a bicycle, bumping into the rear of another child's bicycle—all produce smiles or laughter unless, of course, the child has gotten hurt in the process.

Silly Behavior. A child knocks on the door of a playhouse, and another child opens it in a silly manner. They do this repeatedly, and both laugh every time they do it.

Imagination. A child, playing house, laughs when he tells an adult that he is "in town" and then later that he is "back home." A child pretends to ride horseback, using a broom for a horse. The child laughs when an adult says, "We have a galloping horse here."

Or, in the morning, an adult says "Goodnight" to a child, who replies, "De moon is shining," and laughs.

The Unexpected. Even though not in itself humorous, the unexpected tends to amuse the child of this age. He finds it very funny when things spill, fall, bump, break, or don't work right.

Pretense. Some think it very funny to pretend to cry.

Verbal Humor. Mispronouncing things, such as speaking in a babyish manner when they know better—"goo morning" for "good morning"—amuses them. Or, silly language—"No dumbo! No gumbo!"—seems very funny to most. A few can actually use the word "fun." Or, any unusual word spoken by the adult may be picked up by a child who may not understand it but likes to repeat it humorously.

The child at this age enjoys silly questions asked by the adult. In fact, any silliness or clowning on the part of his parents is very much appreciated.

Many parents find it interesting to be aware of the kinds of things that amuse their child, and to note the way in which humor-providing situations expand and change as the child grows older. Most welcome increasing signs of

humor, as they know that a humorous approach can often help them and their child out of many a tense and tangled situation.

CREATIVITY: VERBAL

Some parents, of course, will not be particularly interested in the following exercise. But if the idea interests you, you might like to try holding your boy or girl on your lap and asking, "Tell me a story." Presumably you will already have told him, or read to him, many stories, so he will know what a story *is*. If he doesn't reply at once, you could prompt him, "What could your story be about?"

If he says, "Baby," or "Little boy," but goes no further, you can prompt him again by asking, "What happened to the little boy?" Chances are that he *will* respond; and, if he doesn't, you can always try again some other day.

Many Two-year-olds do not have enough language or enough desire to respond to a parental request to be very satisfactory storytellers. And if your own Two does not respond, you shouldn't be surprised. Another few months may make a big difference, since by Two-and-a-half many will not only enjoy the activity but may tell you, through what they say, things about themselves and their thinking that you did not know before.

If your child *does* comply and does tell you a story, it will probably be rather short and may be made up of short phrases or sentences. You may be surprised at the amount of violence expressed. Spanking tends to be a leading activity mentioned by girls; falling down and breaking things, by boys. Sometimes it is merely *things* that are broken, but the largest amount of violence occurs to people, very often to the child's own siblings.

Nearly all parents are seen as kind or friendly. Mother is the character predominating in stories by girls, with girls themselves the second leading character. Boys talk mostly about *boys*, with babies a second leading topic.

Stories at Two tend to be characterized by rapid changes of character. Thus, in a single story, the acting character may shift from girl to rabbit to fox to another rabbit to witch. Style is rather jerky, and there are few good transitions. Most stories are laid close to home, and in the majority realism—even though often rather violent realism— predominates.

Children have interesting ways of protecting themselves. They do this by having any bad things that they fantasize about happen to their brothers or sisters, to a child of the opposite sex from their own, or to an animal. Or, if death or illness occurs, it tends to be quickly reversed. Or, broken things are fixed or mended.

A typical *boy* story:

Car. It broke down. It didn't start. Didn't start it. Fix it and it goes. And the engine. I fixed it. Car was cold.

A typical *girl* story, by a rather verbal girl:

About a girl. I think she was frightened by a rabbit. In the woods. He was eating carrots. The rabbit ate the girl all up. Then a fox came out. The fox bited the rabbit. The bunny wanted a west so he wested. Then he woke up again. A witch was coming. She stole the little bunny. He was all eaten by the witch. The witch was killed by a fox. They had to put the witch in jail. First they catch the witches and then they put them in jail. That's all.

At any rate, if you are interested in your own Two-year-old's fantasy life, invite him to tell you a story.

CREATIVITY IN GENERAL

Creativity, of course, does not consist, as some suppose, merely in telling stories or putting on plays or painting. Even the very young child can express his creativity in a great many ways. In addition to the usual painting (or at Two perhaps finger-painting will be more successful), the child can show creativity in his imaginary play.

A box of dress-up clothes gives him a chance to pretend he or she is a grown-up. A box full of colored cloth, buttons, and pipe cleaners permits a combination of materials in creative ways. Big blocks are a prime source of creative combination. Any sort of toy household equipment—doll furniture, doll dishes, doll clothes—allows for doll play that is often extremely creative.

A big box, big enough to climb into, can be a house, a store, a boat, a cave, an airplane—creative imagination often soars, especially at Two-and-a-half, with only the tiniest help from physical properties.

Or, without any props at all, you can ask your child to tell you what he would wish for if he had three wishes. Or, you can ask him to pretend to be a lion, a tiger, a rabbit, a kitten.

Some children are highly creative and imaginative; others more down-to-earth. But even the most factually minded child is likely to show a surprising amount of creativity and imagination if only you can get him started and then are willing to share in his enjoyment.

chapter eight
INDIVIDUALITY

We have been telling you a good deal about the way more or less typical Two-year-olds behave in the many situations that go to make up their daily lives. But don't forget for a minute that every child is in many ways different from every other child, even from his own identical twin.

Not only is every child very much an individual, but each child goes through the usual stages of behavior *at his own rate*. Thus, you may have a highly talkative Two-year-old girl, or you may have a little boy who hardly says much of anything until he is Two-and-a-half or even Three. Small age differences in rate of development should not make you anxious. As long as your Two-year-old seems to understand what is said to him and is able to make his wants known, you shouldn't worry, even if he doesn't talk very much.

For every behavior characteristic known to man, one finds individual differences. Thus, your boy or girl may be highly social and happily responsive to other people, or may be shy and responsive only to those he knows extremely well.

He may welcome new experiences, or may hold back from them; he may do best if warned in advance, or if you spring things on him at the very last minute. He may seem

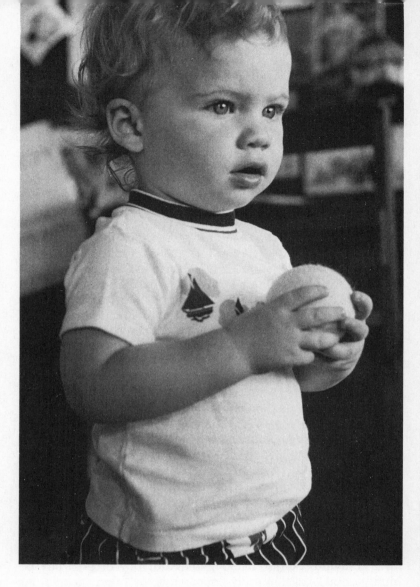

to know his own mind, or may proceed cautiously whatever the situation.

Some protest by producing a full-fledged tantrum. They may squeal, cry, kick, hit, bite, expressing displeasure vigorously and angrily. Others merely frown or whimper or withdraw when things don't go their way.

There are those boys and girls who at the easy ages are very, very easy to get along with, but who at the difficult ages are very, very difficult. There are some who are easy at every age, and some who are difficult at every age. There are those seemingly paradoxical children who are easy at the usual difficult ages and difficult at the expected easy ages.

Or, for some special behavior, such as feeding behavior, Two-year-olds range from those remarkable creatures who can eat with poise (or at least allow themselves to be fed without fuss) at a public restaurant, to those whose feeding habits are so exceptionally immature and troublesome that they cannot even eat at the family table without disrupting the meal.

Not only is every child an individual, with his own very special ways of reacting, but, as Dr. T. Berry Brazelton of Boston points out so effectively,[6] each mother-child couple is also an individual. Some of your children (if you have more than one) will be much easier for you to get along with than will others.

There are some children who, from infancy on, are so easy for their mother to get on with that she very quickly comes to have a feeling of full confidence, which, in turn, adds to the effectiveness of her handling. There are others who just seem to rub their mother the wrong way and who, in turn, react less than smoothly to their mother. This, too, becomes circular, with the mother's lack of success eroding what confidence she may have had to begin with.

It is very important for mothers, and fathers, too, not to blame themselves if one of their children is hard for them to handle. It is important not to take this as a sign that you are not a good parent. Some children are easy for everybody; some are easy for some of the adults in their environment and not for others. Some are difficult for everybody.

So, if your own boy or girl is calmer, or more mature, than those we have described, give yourself some credit, and Nature the rest. If he or she is even more difficult

than the worst we have described, don't blame anyone. Just do your best, try not to lose either patience or confidence, and try to get as much help from others as you can afford and feel that you need.

SEX DIFFERENCES

One very outstanding personality difference that is nearly always observed by parents who have both boys and girls is the difference between the sexes. That differences do exist is generally admitted, though there is considerable question about their actual source. In the past it was assumed that they were inherited. Today, many feel that they are, at least in part, caused by society's expectations, by society's stereotypes.

That is, since in general we expect boys to behave in a generally "boyish" manner, we not only set them this example but reinforce or reward their behavior when they behave in what we consider a properly "boyish" way, and punish or at least disapprove when they behave "girlishly." (And, of course, the same holds true for girls. Though "tomboyish" behavior is not entirely disapproved, many parents talk a lot about things that are or are not "ladylike.")

Today, in many families, these expectations are changing. Many parents take special pains to give their children of either sex the feeling that it is *all right* for boys to behave in a soft or gentle way, for girls to be rough, tough and vigorous. Many who write books for children are taking pains not to perpetuate the usual sexual stereotyping.

It will be interesting to see, as the years go by, what effect this new attitude on the part of adults will actually have on child behavior.

Until a change from sexual stereotyping has been brought about, and regardless of *why* observable differences in the behavior of the two sexes exist, here are some of the differences as we see them today.

Among those most usually accepted are that little girls are easier to raise than are little boys. They tend to be more docile, less aggressive, less rebellious. Also, as a rule, girls develop more rapidly than do boys. They walk earlier, talk earlier, are toilet trained earlier, feed and dress themselves sooner. This earlier development, and especially the ability to express oneself verbally combined with a usually greater interest in other people and a seemingly stronger desire to please, all combine to make girl children in the earliest years easier to raise than boy children.

Small girls not only talk sooner than do small boys, but they also tend to talk more. Girls in general seem more interested in people than in things; boys seem more interested in objects than in people. Boys are often more intense and channelized. Girls seem more diversified in their behavior. Girls, in general, seem definitely more compliant than do boys.

Though sociality is not strong in most Two-year-olds, girls tend to seem somewhat more sociable than boys. And though little boys sometimes do like to play with dolls, in general girls, much more than boys, show a strong interest in doll play. Girls, in general, are quieter than are boys.

Boys in a group seem to have more adjustment difficulties, more quarrels over possessions than do girls. Boys also seem to express more tensional outlets (thumb sucking, biting, masturbating) than do girls.

And even at the early age of Two, rather conspicuous sex differences are seen in the spontaneous stories children tell. Girls mention more people than do boys. Mother is the character most often mentioned by girls, with girls themselves the second leading character. *Boys themselves are the leading characters in stories told by boys.*

Though sex differences in feelings about Mother are not great, boys in stories they tell tend to see their mothers as more friendly than girls do, whereas girls see their fathers in a slightly more favorable light than do boys.

At two as at all other preschool ages, girls, unlike boys, tell more stories that center around notions of socialization than stories that center around the self. Girls also tell longer stories than do boys.

INDIVIDUALITY AS SEEN IN GROUP PLAY

Though most young adults probably will not take this opportunity until they have children of their own, one of the very best ways to observe and to begin to appreciate the tremendous differences among children of the same age is to observe in a nursery school group.

Should you have the chance to watch a group of Two-year-olds, you will perhaps see one child who for weeks clings closely to his mother, barely releasing physical contact. You will see another, who, after only one session or two, releases Mother immediately and strides around the playroom, quite independent.

You will see one who enjoys manipulating objects and materials, but says almost nothing. Another will do very little in the way of actual manipulation, but may keep up quite a running patter, mostly to herself but with now and then a friendly verbal approach to an adult or to other children.

You will see one who seems always on top of the situation, whether in contact with objects or people. Any little problem that arises is easily solved. You will see others who appear to be always in conflict with the world around them. People don't do what they want. Even objects resist.

A little observation in a nursery school or neighborhood play group can do wonders for your morale, for it can suggest—if you will just watch objectively—that the way a child behaves is by no means simply a reflection of "good" or "bad" parenting.

Just remember that every child is born with his or her own individuality. Your handling may make things better or worse, but you do not *produce* your child's basic personality, other than through the genes you gave him!

chapter nine
STORIES FROM REAL LIFE

THE TWO-YEAR-OLD

TWO-YEAR-OLD SUCKS THUMB AND TWISTS HAIR

Dear Doctors:

Our son Jim is now Twenty-six months old. He has sucked his thumb since infancy, and as he got older and his hair grew longer, he began curling and twisting his hair at the same time that he sucked his thumb. When he was Sixteen months old we got him his first boy's haircut. Within three months he was almost bald on the top of his head from this curling business.

I spoke to my doctor about it, but he said it was just a habit and would probably stop. It didn't. We have threatend, sweet-talked, and tried almost everything, but to no avail. We are worried about having a bald Two-year-old.

People tell us he must be lacking something, but for the life of me I can't figure out what. Maybe it seems to him that I'm picking on him too much, but he is very active and devilish and does need a lot of correcting.

Jim's is a hard combination to beat. Mothers whose children suck their thumbs and at the same time fondle a blanket often dislike the habit, but in a way they are fortunate. Not only is it sometimes possible later on, as the need for this relief diminishes, to get the blanket away from the child, but also you don't mind the wear and tear on the blanket as much as you do the wear and tear on your child's hair. (Or on his ear, which he may pull; or his nose, which he may scratch.)

Your doctor is undoubtedly right. This behavior *will* stop eventually, though before it stops for good it may have several spells of seeming temporarily to be better and then getting worse again.

An extremely short haircut might help make it harder for your son to get hold of his hair. Girls will sometimes accept wearing a soft angora bonnet, so that they pull at the fuzz on the bonnet and not at their hair. A little boy might accept some masculine type of head covering at night, though probably not in the daytime.

You might be able to get your son interested in a soft toy animal with fuzz that he can pull. However, it is actually the tension in his own head that he is probably trying to relieve, so that pulling the fuzz off a toy may not help much. What really needs to be done is to relieve some of the tension he feels. Try giving him more time away from his older sister, more time alone with you. Good, active outdoor play may help. Nursery school attendance, in another few months, might unscramble some of his tensions.

As with most of these undesirable habits that parents want to get rid of, it is usually best to concentrate not on the habit itself but rather on the tensions that produce it.

IMPROVED BEDTIME ROUTINE
DIMINISHES NIGHT FEARS

Dear Doctors:

Hopefully other mothers of children with night fears might be helped by my story of our little daughter, who had been switched from her crib to a regular bed shortly after her second birthday, to make way for her baby sister. About the same time she had bronchitis, her temperature soared, and in her delirium she saw something which scared her.

Shortly after that, she began insisting that there was a cow who came to her bedroom after she had gone to bed. We could hear her sweet little voice intoning, "Cow not get me, cow not get me," more to convince herself than us.

I considered the move from crib to bed—probably from her point of view the crib bars were not to keep her in but to keep other things out. I considered the delirium— perhaps it had been a cow that frightened her in her dream.

So we talked and reassured her, provided a night light, became personally acquainted with some real cows at Grandpa's farm, and talked and reassured some more. Still the cow came nightly. I took her up in my arms one night and said, "I don't see any cow. Show me the cow."

"Right there," she said and pointed to her empty crib across the room.

Finally, quite by chance, I stumbled onto the real reason for the cow. Our nightly routine was to bathe and put on pajamas, read a story, go to bed, get up to go to potty, go to bed, get up for a drink, go to bed, get up to look out into the living room—you've heard it a thousand times.

Eventually, nearly every night, I had to become cross. But, on nights when we parted on good terms, there was no cow.

So our routine changed. After that, when she had made that last trip out to the living room, I took her back to bed, tucked her in, then lay down across her bed and we talked. I told her what a dear little girl she was, how much we loved her, how happy we were to have her— and, "It's time to go to sleep now." I didn't mention the cow—and neither did she. And soon the cow left our house forever.

TWO-YEAR-OLD TAKES TEDDY BEAR TO BED WITH HER

Dear Doctors:

Perhaps you wouldn't even consider mine a problem, but my little girl, Patty, just two, has developed almost an obsession for a little teddy bear that she calls "Baby." Patty is a rather thin child, blond, very active, but a poor eater. She has a little brother Eight months old now, and she seems to love him very much. I have tried to show her extra love and affection since the new baby came so she wouldn't be jealous of him.

She has always been quite a sleeping problem, probably because when she was a baby I never was firm, but used to hold her and rock her to sleep. She never sucked her thumb or paid much attention to her toys. She gave up her bottle at Nine months, took it back after the baby was born, then gave it up again all by herself at Eighteen months.

Since she has become so attached to "Baby," she'll take him to bed with her and is no trouble at all. My girl friend thinks you shouldn't allow a child to take any toys to bed with her, that a child should go to bed and just sleep. Patty surrounds herself with toys and plays for an hour or more before she falls asleep. Am I wrong in allowing her to do this?

Also, to get back to "Baby," she won't even go to the bathroom without him. She won't eat without him. No matter what other toys she plays with, he is always next to her. She just clings to him so hard all the time. Is it normal for a child to be so attached to a toy, or is something lacking—as my friend says?

You have given an excellent description of the strength and importance of the preschooler's customary attachment to some stuffed animal, doll, or even sometimes to just a blanket or piece of cloth. Routines of going to sleep, eating, being dressed or changed can often be almost incredibly simplified if the child is allowed the presence of this favorite object.

Needless to say, we do not agree with your girl friend's objection to this teddy bear. Nor can we agree that a child "should go to bed and just sleep." Fine if he would, but your experience shows that without such a comforter bed-time can indeed be a problem.

GRANDMOTHER WORRIES—HER TWO-YEAR-OLD GRANDSON IS NOT TOILET TRAINED

Dear Doctors:

What can I do about my daughter? She is a good housekeeper and a wonderful mother in all respects but one. Her little boy is Two years old now, and he is not toilet trained yet, either day or night. When I talk to her about it and try to make her see how serious this is, she pays no attention, just goes right on making no effort to train him. Believe me, I am very heartsick and ashamed about this whole thing.

You are by no means alone in your complaint. In fact, your worry seems to be such a common one among the older generation that we'd like to say a few words on behalf of the young mothers of today who are, it is true, not work-ing at the business of toilet training the way their own mothers did a generation ago.

The current policy is not to start in with efforts to train a child for daytime dryness until he or she seems nearly ready to respond to such training. This policy is in keeping with current knowledge, widely presented by child psychol-ogists and pediatricians, that children learn things best, and training is most effective, when they are mature enough to perform the expected task or activity. Training of any kind given before the child is ready to respond is for the most part ineffective, useless, and a wasted expenditure of energy.

Suppose that the child is going to be ready for daytime dryness around Two years of age. You may find him noticing wetness. You may find that his span is increasing, so that he customarily wakes up dry from his nap. These are signs that he is about ready to be able to stay dry. Then and only then are a mother's efforts to keep him dry going to be effective.

But suppose that a given child is a little slow in developing. Say that according to his time schedule dryness is not really going to come in until around Thirty months of age. If his conscientious mother starts in when he is around Eighteen months old to try to train him, older relatives may feel that she is doing her duty. But actually she is probably not only wasting time but may be building up real resistance. With such a child, one might as well wait until he is almost Two-and-a-half.

That is, the child's readiness, not the efforts of his mother, is the major factor in determining success in toilet training. But any mother needs to be aware, after her child is Two years old, of methods to which he might best respond. There should be some trial-and-error, some giving of an idea to the child without pushing. (Very often a potty chair is preferred to the big toilet with a toidy seat attached.)

You as a grandmother do have something on your side, but we think your daughter, in waiting, is wisely following the growth needs of her own child.

BOYS OFTEN SLOWER IN TALKING THAN GIRLS

Dear Doctors:

I have a question which I hope you can answer to set my mind at ease. My son, aged Twenty-seven months, is very active, strong and healthy, bright and intelligent. He is toilet trained and eats and sleeps nicely. However, I am concerned because he doesn't seem to be talking.

He says some words such as "daddy," "bus," "bird," "dog," etc., but not clearly, omitting the sound of the first letter, so that what he actually says is "urd," "og." He jabbers away in what he seems to think are sentences. When he points to anything, we clearly say the name of the thing first to him before giving it to him.

He makes us know he wants to go to the bathroom by taking us there, and if he wants a glass of milk he goes to the refrigerator and gets the milk bottle and proceeds to pour himself a glass of milk. He understands everything said to him and in fact seems exceptionally bright in this respect.

He also understands the daily routine of the household and constantly amazes us by the little things he does that we hadn't thought a child of his age could be doing. Can you tell me from all this if I do have a problem with my son's lack of talking in clear sentences, or if this jabbering of his is what normally precedes talking?

We can set your mind at ease, at least as far as it is possible to make a diagnosis without seeing the child in question. Certainly, from everything you say, your son sounds like a good, bright little boy who is developing normally. His language is a little bit slow, but this is not unusual in boys. Jargoning (jabbering in a conversational manner) normally comes in at around Eighteen to Twenty-one months. He is Twenty-seven months, and thus a little behind the average.

But we can assure you that many perfectly normal boys do not say very much, sometimes until they are well into Three years of age. There is nothing in your letter that causes us to be concerned about your son's development. His comprehension and his ways of making his wants known sound perfectly normal.

FATHER FEELS GUILTY BECAUSE HE GETS TIRED OF PLAYING WITH HIS TWO-YEAR-OLD SON

Dear Doctors:

I have what is developing into a serious problem with my Two-and-a-half-year-old son Dennis, and I sometimes doubt my ability to cope with it. Dennis is, so far, an only child. Because he has very little access to other children his age, and because I must of necessity be away from him a good deal, I seem to spend most of my waking, nonworking hours playing with him. Or at least so it seems to me. I read to him, build blocks with him, play ball with him, and engage in many other activities which he finds pleasurable.

Our problem arises out of my extreme agitation over Dennis's lack of interest in playing alone when I am home, and a concomitant fear I have of telling him "No" when I don't want to play. I find it nearly impossible to enter into play without manifesting my resentment when I didn't want to play in the first place; and I am sure he finds this attitude of mine disturbing.

I so hate to say "No" to him, and I find myself saying it more and more. But what else can I say when I feel "No" and cannot hide it? As it turns out, the more I say "No," either covertly or overtly, the more he strives for a positive "Yes" from me. Is it possible for a Twenty-seven-month-old boy to realize that his too-often-absent dad can sometimes say "No" to his play demands and still not be rejecting him?

We fear that, like many conscientious and responsible young parents today, you are letting your preschooler make too many demands. And you are taking them too seriously and feeling guilty when you can't, or don't want to, give in to them.

Boys like Dennis can be very hard to cope with, especially for a conscientious parent. It looks as though you will have to have a more scheduled life so far as he is concerned. And here is where his mother needs to think through his total day and set up a good schedule for his being with you, and being away from you.

This is the kind of boy who needs, if possible, to live in a house big enough so that you, his father, can at times get away from him. Then you will plan certain times when you are definitely going to be with him fully. You would feel better about the whole thing if you knew that your time with him was to be limited. Then you wouldn't feel guilty the rest of the time, and he wouldn't be usurping your life the way he is.

This kind of child often does best with one person alone with him at a time. In the midst of the family group he tends to create chaos. A good relationship with a responsible baby-sitter could do much to relieve the pressure on you.

REMARKABLE TWO-YEAR-OLD LESS REMARKABLE AT FOUR

Dear Doctors:

I thought other mothers might like to hear about my own son, who at Two seemed to us so very advanced. Billy is now Four, but he showed his superiority early. He has a fantastic memory, now quoting conversations that took place two years ago.

I know how other mothers of children who show superiority feel—pride, amazement, yet some anxiety and fear. How to keep up with them? However, the problem is not as great as some think. With my boy I found that his very rapid learning kept on until he was Three, and *then tapered off*. At the rate he was going, I thought he would be reading by Three, but that part of learning took a slump, and only now, at Four-and-a-half, is he showing any slight signs of reading.

He can use a typewriter, hunt-and-peck. He tries to bang out nursery rhymes on his toy piano. He is bright and alert, but it is not so noticeable nor so frightening as it was two years ago. I daresay that two years hence he will have evened out still more as compared to other bright children of his age.

Your good letter confirms our frequent observation that many children who are almost frighteningly intelligent around Two or so, while not losing their superiority, do tend to level off somewhat as they grow older.

Thus, a Two-year-old who is two years advanced and who behaves like a Four-year-old (if such a child exists) would rate an IQ of 200. A Five-year-old who is two years advanced rates much lower.

Certainly we anticipate that your son will always be a bright boy and will probably do extremely well in school. But it is also true, as you have observed, that often a rather startling acceleration in a Two-year-old does level off considerably by the time the child is Four or Five.

Your letter can be helpful to other mothers of early-bright children who tend to worry about how to provide for them all the intellectual food they "need" in their earliest years, or who worry because they think they have potential geniuses on their hands.

HOW TO TELL TWO-YEAR-OLD ABOUT DEATH OF HIS BROTHER?

Dear Doctors:

Because you are so understanding of the stages of development, I hope you can help me handle a situation without causing some trauma.

Briefly, we should like to know how to tell our Twenty-two-month-old son that before he was born we had another little boy who died at the age of Fourteen months. We feel it will be better for him to grow up knowing, rather than at the age of five or so to hear it from some other child or unthinking adult. We are afraid that he might, if the situation is not handled right, feel that someday he might die or that we might get another baby to replace him.

We don't believe you can simply tell a child he has a little brother in Heaven. When my mother died, I was Ten, and was told that, and for years I had nightmares of searching for her in this frightening place called "Heaven."

At what age should we tell him? Is it possible that because of our own emotions we are exaggerating this matter?

It is too soon to tell your boy about the death of his little brother. In fact, as you yourself suggest, you are quite possibly exaggerating the problem because of your own natural emotions in the matter.

We believe that at a considerably later date the opportunity to tell him about his brother will come about perfectly naturally. You might, for instance, be showing him pictures of relatives and the baby's picture might be among them.

If your son had known his brother, there might be a reason to talk about him. But since he did not know him, there is no special reason to suppose that the information will be of tremendous importance to him now.

All of this quite naturally seems like a big problem to you because it means so much to you. But children are often quite coldhearted, especially about things that don't affect them personally. A brother in Heaven probably will mean no more to your son than a grandmother or grandfather who may have died before he was born.

TWO-AND-A-HALF YEARS

GIRL IS A FEEDING PROBLEM

Dear Doctors:

My Two-and-a-half-year-old daughter Magda is a feeding problem. She was doing a really rather good job of feeding herself, or at least trying to, until her twin brothers were born. Now she not only won't try to feed herself—except the things she likes most—but her diet is extremely restricted. Should I continue to help her in order that she will get a balanced diet? Will my feeding her, at this rather late age, hinder her and make her transition to feeding herself again even more difficult? At what age, and just how, shall I go about getting her to feed herself once again?

It sounds as if until the boys were born Magda was doing a rather good job of her eating. It is not too remarkable, at this difficult age of Two-and-a-half, that with twin siblings younger than she, your daughter would be balking somewhere. Since eating has apparently always been one of her weaker spots, it is quite natural that here would be your difficulty.

You say that she will feed herself the foods she likes best. There is no reason why you shouldn't feed her the other foods you want her to eat. With most children you don't decide arbitrarily just when they are old enough to feed themselves entirely. You just wait and see how things turn out. The less you make of the whole thing, the more casually you feed her things she won't eat by herself, the less of a problem you should experience, and the sooner the whole matter should resolve itself.

BOY WON'T STAY IN BED

Dear Doctors:

I have a problem with my Two-and-a-half-year-old son Eric. For the last month I haven't been able to get him to stay in bed. We had gotten him a Hollywood bed, and he enjoyed being able to get out of bed by himself. Now he abuses that privilege. I keep him up later now, but the minute I put him into bed and leave him, he comes right out of his room with a cheerful, "Hi, Mommy." This he can keep up a dozen times.

I have tried every means I can think of to make him stay in bed. I've explained to him, I've told him stories, I've sung to him. And, much as I hate to do it, I have even threatened him, licked him, made him stand in the corner, and even locked the door for a minute or two.

If we leave him alone and let him keep his door open, he climbs out of bed, then gets his shoes, socks, book, and takes them back to bed with him.

There is something else, too. Several times a week

he wakes up in the night. When he gets up, he goes and lies down on the dog's bed. He doesn't wake me up, but usually a second sense does wake me and I put him back into bed. He'll stay in his bed about ten or fifteen minutes, and then he does the same thing over again. Sometimes he keeps this up for a couple of hours.

Could you please help me with these problems? I am really desperate. I don't know what to do anymore, and I'm expecting a second child.

Children often have difficulty in staying in bed at this age, but generally the going-to-bed routine has settled down *before* the roaming-in-the-middle-of-the-night starts. You are getting a double dose of sleeping problems.

At Two-and-a-half, it is often possible to build up a going-to-bed routine, and to go over it with the child each night. Perhaps you can have certain things that he associates just with going to sleep, such as his bottle, since he still takes one, or perhaps some special book, such as *Goodnight Moon.* Sometimes a woolly animal helps the child to stay in bed. Or, you could put some of his favorite possessions into his bed before you put him to bed.

As for his middle-of-the-night wanderings, try tying his door loosely with a stocking or some stretchy material (tie the stocking to the knob and to something secure nearby so that he can open the door only a few inches but can't get out of his room).

If going-to-bed problems are very bad, sometimes they are solved most quickly by having someone other than the mother put the child to bed, and by having the mother actually out of the house at bedtime. Often this doesn't take more than a week or two.

Many parents find that the child is not really ready to be moved to the big bed until he is Four and can be expected to stay in bed all night. You have made the move, however, and are experiencing all the joys of night wandering. Since Eric finds it so hard to remain in his own bed, you might provide a good alternate bed on the floor. Then you could start him to bed in this alternate bed. Or, he can start in his own bed and move when he feels like it.

Knowing that he probably isn't going to stay in his own bed, if alternatives seem too difficult, you could move his mattress onto the floor. Barricade it with blocks or boxes to make a cozy enclosure.

We don't know exactly what will work with Eric, but try to be flexible in your planning. It really does no harm if he doesn't spend the entire night in his very own bed. Most outgrow this need to roam after a brief spell. And most outgrow it more quickly if you don't fight it.

TWO-AND-A-HALF-YEAR-OLD BITES

Dear Doctors:

I am in frantic need of help. My Two-and-a-half-year-old daughter Jane has me baffled. She is very active and an only child, though not a jealous one. She bites other children for no reason at all. Not just small bites. She bites terribly hard until she draws blood. Always it is children younger than she, even small babies. This has been going on for over a year now.

I have tried biting her back, spanking, making her sit on a chair through the rest of a visit, but she still continues to bite. I just don't know what to do next. We are expecting a new baby soon and must correct this biting before the baby comes.

My husband says not to take her visiting anymore. But we just can't discard all our friends because of this problem. We've tried everything. Please help.

Actually, both you and your husband are right. You can't give up all your friends because your daughter bites. However, Jane is showing by her behavior that she is not old enough to be taken visiting as you have been doing.

Biting is usually an indication that a social situation is making too great demands on the young biter. Isolation and a simpler play situation often will reduce biting. These are the most recommended approaches. Try to figure out what about the situation is making such excessive demands on your daughter that she has to express herself by biting, and then try to reduce these demands.

However, biting, like spitting, is an unusually unpopular behavior—not only with those bitten but with adults as well. It makes us want to do something, and something violent, at once. (Perhaps it arouses instinctive fears in us, or memories of our own bitten childhoods.)

Many parents and nursery school teachers have found that if they can manage to watch a biter carefully enough to anticipate biting, then, as he or she starts to bite, if they cup a hand under the child's chin and quickly and firmly snap his mouth shut, this stops the act of biting and may cause him to bite his own tongue. This stratagem has been known to discourage many biters.

Better than this, can't you arrange to do more of your visiting when your daughter is in bed? Can you afford a baby-sitter when you need to visit in the daytime? Or, when visiting, can you devote more attention to your daughter and her play? She is obviously not mature enough at this time to go visiting and then be left, unsupervised, to play with other children or babies.

This biting is not so much "badness" as immaturity. It will undoubtedly get better as she grows older. We must admit, though, that an aggressive little girl like yours may continue to get into trouble if allowed to play, unsupervised, for sometime to come. Aggressiveness does have its advantages as a child grows older, but in the early years it can make for a lot of trouble.

TWO-AND-A-HALF-YEAR-OLD WON'T KEEP HER CLOTHES ON

Dear Doctors:

Our youngest child is Two-and-a-half. Our problem is trying to keep her clothes on her. She is almost completely toilet trained. At first when she took her shoes and socks off, it was because they were damp and she wanted us to know she was uncomfortable.

Now, however, if we put a dress on her, she refuses to wear a sweater, or to keep her underpants on. The first thing I know, off comes everything.

I have been firm, and even made a game of it, but after a while she repeats the procedure all over again. The floors here are not heated, and this could prove very harmful to her. As for overalls, dungarees, or anything that covers her legs, she just won't hear of them. Fortunately, she will stay covered at night.

Undressing and running around without any clothes on is not an unusual preschool behavior. It probably occurs most around Twenty-one months. Two-and-a-half is a little late. When it goes on as long as this, the most effective move is to prevent it. Prevent it not by telling the child not to take her clothes off, not by spanking, but by arranging her clothes in such a way that she just plain cannot get them off.

Regardless of how she may feel about them, coveralls put on backward usually do the trick. Ordinary zippers or fasteners will probably be adequate, but if they are not, pin or even baste the coveralls on. (In this instance, since your daughter doesn't like to have anything over her legs, these may be short coveralls.) Tie shoelaces in double bows. Most Two-and-a-half-year-olds can't get these untied.

However, it would do no harm and might make her happier if she could have a special time and place when she could take her clothes off and run around—perhaps just before her bath.

Also, it would be a good idea to check over the past few weeks and figure out if this behavior tends to take place at any special time of day. It often turns out that a child behaves this way when she has become overtired, at the end of the morning or afternoon. If that is the case, this can be a clue to you to try to arrange her schedule so that this overfatigue need not occur.

GIRL A COMBINATION OF ALL THE NAUGHTY CHILDREN THAT
EVER WERE

Dear Doctors:

My problem is my Two-and-a-half-year-old daughter
Penny. She seems to be a combination of all the naughty
children I've ever read about. I am at a complete loss
as to how to handle her and am losing all confidence in
myself.

Here are some of the things she does. For instance,
while I try to eat or clean up or do anything at all, she's
simply into something different every second. For example:

1. She runs in and turns on TV full force after putting
the plug into the wall herself. 2. Turns on gas jets and
runs. 3. Unlocks front door and runs out into rain, snow,
or cold. 4. Runs upstairs, grabs one end of the toilet
paper, and dashes madly around the room. Always throws
anything handy into the toilet and flushes it. 5. Sticks
bobby pins into wall sockets. 6. Takes plugs from all
wall sockets and removes OFF and ON switches from the
lamps, making it impossible to use them until these
tiny stems are found. Takes bulbs from sockets and has
had many a good shock from sticking her fingers down
there. 7. Takes telephone off hook. When she sees me
coming, she giggles, throws receiver down, and runs like
mad. 8. Pulls the drapes so hard she bends the curtain
rods. 9. Writes on walls if she can find a stray pencil
or can get one by climbing on drainboard and reaching
into cabinet above it. 10. Grabs our small dog and jams
pencils, toys, or food down her throat—twists her ears,
pinches her, and then says "Sorry" and gives the dog
a kiss. 11. Washes anything she sees with rag dunked
in dog's water or toilet bowl. 12. Opens refrigerator door
every chance she gets and eats anything she can grab.
13. Pulls leaves off my plants and throws them on the
floor.

Now you may think (as others have) that she does

only a few of these things each day; but it is continuous, all day long. It is impossible for me to do *any* housework.

Penny is funny and can be sweet and loving, but she has me worn out with her everlasting energy. Friends have offered to watch her for me while I made a trip to the dentist or such, but when I come back (after only an hour) they flop in a chair and say, "How can you ever stand it? Boy! You have to watch her every second!" They never offer again.

In desperation I took her to my doctor. He observed her for some time and gave the following diagnosis: a healthy, intelligent, hyperactive, mischievous, devilish, persistent, teasing child, approximately a year beyond her age. He suggested a tranquilizing drug given three times a day. It did no good. It only made her stumble and bump into things as she traveled her mischievous rounds.

Should I take her to a child psychologist? Or, can you suggest any ways to discipline her?

What you, or any mother of such a superactive meso-morphic preschooler, need is not so much advice as at least one (if not more) individual with a strong character and quick reflexes who will spell you in the constant supervision and care that Penny needs. Lacking that, or in addition to that, check on what nursery schools are available in your community. Your daughter is not too young to go to nursery school three mornings a week.

Next, hire someone to take her out for two or three hours every afternoon, or have that person stay at home with her while you go out yourself. Also, a fortunate choice of play-mates often helps. A slightly older boy may find a little girl like yours quite interesting to play with.

Third, get as many secure locks as possible to protect medications and dangerous (or fragile) items in your house from this predatory little girl. Put other things as high as possible. Give her a good supply of materials that she can legitimately be messy with, that she can legitimately pound or destroy—clay, Play-Doh, paint, sand, water. Provide her with as much equipment as possible as an outlet of gross motor energy—Jungle Gym, slide, bouncing board, doorway swing.

Fourth, take courage in the fact that she will not always be so destructive and so demanding of time and energy.

If finances permit, a summer or part of a summer at the beach could help out. The seashore provides space, the excitement of the waves, and fewer things that can be damaged. It does have a calming effect on many of these supervigorous children.

Do not give up on medication. Penny is young for this, but just because the dosage that your doctor recommended was excessive does not mean that no help is possible from drugs.

Lastly—in answer to your question about the psychologist or clinic—certainly we feel that any parent will, or should, understand a boy or girl better after the child has had a thorough developmental examination and personality appraisal at a qualified child-guidance clinic. But even the best clinic, like your own physician, can give no magic formula for slowing down a high-drive, mesomorphic preschooler. In a family where money may not be too plentiful, we would be inclined to suggest spending any available funds on getting someone to take turns with you in the care of such an active, aggressive child instead of spending it on professional help.

ROCKING MAY BE SIGN OF GENERAL OVERACTIVITY

Dear Doctors:

I have a Two-and-a-half-year-old son, Chad, who every night rocks his crib. We have put a thick rug under it, and this cuts down on the noise and movement of the crib. But his activity seems to us excessive.

Also, he is a head banger. We try to reduce any possible hurt or damage by encouraging him to bang on a soft rug or carpet, but he seems to prefer hard surfaces. I have read in some of your earlier books that these behaviors are not necessarily harmful, but they worry us. Will you comment?

Our position has been that in a great many young children both head banging and crib rocking may fairly be considered just an extreme example of what we call tensional outlets. That is, the child feels tension, and each relieves it in his own way. Some suck their thumbs, some pull out their hair, some bang their heads, some rock their beds. In some, these last two may have no more serious significance than thumb sucking, which most of us take pretty calmly these days.

In fact, crib rocking is thought by some to have its distinctly positive side. It seems to occur in many children who have good rhythm and possibly even real musical ability.

However, a more serious note enters the picture. Such an authority as Dr. Ben Feingold of California, in his lively book *Why Your Child Is Hyperactive*,[7] suggests that in some instances either rocking or head banging may be an early sympton of hyperkinesis (overactivity).

This, of course, at least in its extreme forms, *is* harmful, causing child and family, and later on his school, vast difficulty.

Happily, hyperactivity can be reduced if need be—at least in many children—with drugs. Better still, some authorities, like Dr. Feingold, believe that proper diet— especially removal from the child's diet of all artificial coloring and flavoring—can not only control but often put an end to such hyperactivity.

So, continue putting a soft rug under Chad's crib. Keep on encouraging him to bang his head on soft surfaces. But also read Dr. Feingold's book and consider the importance of a careful supervision of Chad's or any other young child's, diet.

DIFFICULT BOY

Dear Doctors:

My Two-and-a-half-year-old son Danny is an awful problem. Not a day goes by without fights, hollering, and spankings. He seems to have all children's problems rolled into one. Recently he has turned into a mean, snarling child. If anyone speaks to him, he snarls at them and screams "No!" which is his answer to everything. It is a battle to dress him, wash him, or take him anywhere.

One thing that especially bothers me is his indecision. He won't decide things for himself or let me decide for him, either. He will tell me he has to go to the bathroom and then run into the other room and wait for me to chase him. Or, he will ask for something, and, when I offer it to him, will say, "No, I don't want it." If I say, "All right, don't take it," he will carry on as if I had beat him. He is like this about everything. The more I spank him for things, the more determined he seems to do them.

Most dinner hours are just a fight to the finish when his father is home, though if we are alone at lunch I can get most anything into him by letting him play, with me spooning the food into his mouth. My husband and I don't agree about discipline—he is more strict than I am.

People have told me they have never seen a more active child or a more stubborn one. We have had to build a top for his crib to cage him in.

Nearly everything you say about your son paints an almost classic picture of Two-and-a-half. You need to recognize that a child of this age tends to be at his worst (or at his best) with his mother. And no matter how well you discipline, this kind of behavior is likely to occur.

Two-and-a-half is by nature rigid, ritualistic, and negative. Almost anything you want the child to do, he doesn't

127

do. And every single item of the day's routine is likely to become a matter for resistance. You have merely to make any wish or plan of your own known, and he sets his wish or plan against it.

Understanding the behavior typical of this age may help, but don't just accept it. Figure out ways and means to by-pass or work through it. Try using some of the techniques listed on pages 29 to 39. Definitely get somebody else to take over the care of your son for part of every day if possible.

The fact that he eats better for you alone suggests that it may work best, with your son, to simplify things as much as possible, and, if you can, have only one adult present during basic routines.

If you and your husband can't agree about discipline, have Father take over some areas of discipline, and you take others.

Rough, tough boys like yours are often good about domestic activities. Try to have him do this sort of thing along with you. And definitely, even if he can't have a real nap, give him and yourself the relief that comes from the time apart provided by a play nap every afternoon.

HELPING CHILD ADJUST TO ARRIVAL OF NEW BABY

Dear Doctors:

My husband and I are expecting our second child. Our problem is the usual one of how to adjust our Two-and-a-half-year-old to the baby. We want to make sure to avoid any jealousy or unhappiness or feelings of displacement, but we don't know just how to go about all this.

You can't be certain to avoid all jealousy or unhappiness or feelings of displacement, but you *can* make the usual efforts in this direction. Since you cannot predict what any given child's reactions will be, you can only use your best common sense and feel your way.

First, don't tell him about the baby too soon. A month

in advance should be plenty unless he notices your increasing size and asks questions. Second, don't exaggerate about how much fun the baby is going to be and how great it is going to be to have it around. Possibly the less said, the better.

Most important is to make good plans for his comfort and security while you are gone. Some do best with a familiar sitter right in their own home. Others miss Mother less if they go to Grandmother's or some other relative's home.

Some find it helpful, on the baby's return or just before, if the older child is given a present, supposedly from the baby. This seems rather extreme to us, but it might work—presents have great power. Many recommend that whenever friends bring presents for the baby they give the older child a present, too. This can get cumbersome, and it might be best if all present-giving is played down.

The most important thing is to arrange as well as you can that the Two-year-old's life is not too terribly disrupted by the arrival of the baby. Obviously, Mother's time will be rather well occupied. But it works out very well if she can still plan to spend as much time as possible with the older child, and have any sitter or other help take over the baby whenever practical.

And if the child at times expresses hostility to the baby or asks you to take it back to the hospital, such feelings should be accepted and respected, even though he will eventually have to appreciate that the baby is here to stay.

CHILD WAKES UP EARLY AND BEHAVES BADLY

Dear Doctors:

My problem is my Two-and-a-half-year-old son Joey, who gets up at 7:00 A.M. or earlier (before I get up) and gets into the bathroom and makes an awful mess with soap and water and such. I have everything else put up where he can't reach it, but the water and soap must be there. He puts everything he can find down the toilet.

This morning he went downstairs, and you can imagine —sugar, salt, cereal, coffee, honey, everything all mixed up and spilled everywhere.

He is so quiet about it, I never wake up. My alarm goes off at eight, and he used to sleep until then, but no longer. He is very bright for his age, talks well, eats poorly. I am a widow, and it's hard bringing up a child without a father. I hope you can help me.

We sympathize fully with your wish for a little more sleep in the morning, and also for your wish that your son behave while you are getting this sleep. Unfortunately, like other mothers of preschoolers, you are probably going to have to choose between sleep and the preservation of your property. We suspect you are going to have to set *your* alarm for seven.

In another six months you may find that by putting out a little food or some toys or picture books you can keep him happy in his own room for a short while after he wakes. But until then, you might try tying his door with a bell that will warn you when he is up as he tries to open the door.

It is the dream of many a mother to be able just to lie there and sleep while her young child entertains himself quietly and harmlessly until she is ready to wake. As a rule, however, she gets her sleep at the expense of finding the house strewn with things like salt, cereal, coffee, and honey, if not with broken glass.

True, you can't put everything out of reach. But perhaps you could lock a few more doors and cupboards. As far as the bathroom is concerned, you *could* put the soap in the medicine chest. Better yet, a high hook on the door would keep him out except when you could be with him.

VICKY DOES OPPOSITE OF WHAT SHE IS TOLD

Dear Doctors:

I have gotten into rather a mess with my Two-and-a-half-year-old daughter Vicky. At first I thought the whole thing was rather amusing, and clever on my part. Now I am not so sure.

It started with my discovering that when I wanted Vicky to do something she didn't want to do, she would not do it unless I told her to do just the opposite of what I really wanted. Thus, if I see that she is playing with her food and is not interested in eating, I say, "Vicky, don't eat your lunch all up because I want some of it," she will finish in two seconds.

This was all very well at first and seemed to simplify life. But now it has gotten so she will hardly do a thing unless I tell her to do its opposite, and I feel that this is somewhat not right.

Your experience is fairly common. It is true that many children at Two-and-a-half are so very contrary that they prefer to do exactly the opposite of what they are told. Other mothers, like you, have discovered that you can get them to do what you want by telling them not to do it. Or vice versa.

This *does* work. The trouble is, as you have found, it can very quickly get to be too much of a good thing, so many mothers prefer not to start it. Now that you are in a trap of your own making, you may find that in order to break this pattern you will do best not to give direct commands, such as, "Do this," or, "Don't do that." Instead, try using the usual preschool techniques of, "How about having your snack now?," or, "Let's pick up your toys."

The general advantage of such techniques is that if the child does not follow your suggestion you can skip the whole thing and no face is lost. In your case, the advantage will be that since no specific order is given, it will be harder for Vicky to do the opposite.

CHILDREN WON'T PLAY WITH TWO-AND-A-HALF-YEAR-OLD

Dear Doctors:

My Two-and-a-half-year-old just can't seem to play successfully with his friends. With children of his own age, he is so aggressive that play always ends up in a fight. With older children, he always gets the worst of it and ends up crying, so they don't find him much fun. How can I help him to do better at play?

Clearly, since your child right now can't solve his own social problems, you do need to help out. To begin with, figure which (and how many) of the other children your son gets on best with and then try to have him play chiefly with them. Numbers make a difference. Some children can play well with one other child but not with two or three.

Time, too, makes a difference. Some can play quite harmoniously for fifteen or twenty minutes but not longer. Place matters, too. Some feel safer on home ground and can play well at home but not elsewhere. Others seem to have too many possessions to defend at home, and do better at another's house. Still others do best in a neutral area, such as a park or playground.

Most of all, you can help with supervision. And here you may do something that doesn't work as well at later ages. You can call up other mothers and make arrangements for play. Each mother will probably give what supervision is needed in her own home. But when it is a matter of outdoor play, sometimes mothers in a neighborhood do plan together quite successfully to take turns to see that some adult is always available. The amount of direct supervision will vary with the neighborhood situation, but a mother at hand can often make a great deal of difference.

Two-and-a-half can be a rather stormy age socially. But with help from Mother, almost any Two-and-a-half-year-old can avoid being a total social failure.

EPILOGUE

So, mothers and fathers, that is your Two-year-old, at least as we have seen him. And if, during the latter part of this important year, your little boy or girl sometimes seems a bit difficult, a bit demanding, more than a bit rigorous and rigid and hard to handle than before, remember that growth cannot always go smoothly.

Your child will, with added age, grow larger and more capable and increasingly independent. But the upward path of growing is not always smooth, and there will inevitably come times when any child is somewhat tangled within himself and somewhat difficult in his relationships with those around him.

Fortunately in most instances, behavior does develop in a patterned way, so that we, and you, can within reason know what to expect.

One of the things *we* expect is that even if things may sometimes have been difficult for you *and* your offspring as he moved from Two on into Three, at least during the first half of the year now to come he or she should, with luck, be as comfortable and conforming, as friendly and fun, as even the most optimistic parent could wish.

APPENDIXES
Equipment and Toys Suitable Throughout the Preschool Years

Animals, toy
Baskets and boxes
Boards and sawhorse for see-saw
Boards for balancing and sliding
Bouncing board
Broom, dustpan, mop, dust-cloth
Brushes for painting
Chest of drawers, cupboard
Clay
Climbing apparatus, such as Jungle Gym, Tower Gym, ladders, boxes
Costume box, including pocket-books, hats, gloves, scarves, jewelry, curtains
Crayons, large-size
Dishes and cooking utensils
Doll bed
Doll carriage
Doll clothing, with large buttons and buttonholes
Easel
Easel paper

Hand puppets
Hollow blocks
Kegs
Laundry tub, ironing board, iron, adult-size clothespins
Logs
Musical instruments, such ·as wrist bells, drum, dinner gong, xylophone, music box
Nature specimens, such as fish, turtles, salamanders, rabbits, guinea pigs, or plants
Nests of boxes or cans
Packing boxes, large and sturdy enough for a child to climb on
Paint—powder paint mixed with water
Phonograph
Rope and string
Sandbox
Sand toys, including sugar scoop, pail, cans, sifter
Slide
Small airplanes, automobiles, trucks, boats, trains

Small boards for building, hauling

Stove

Suitcases

Table and chair, child-size

Train, dump truck, steam shovel, large enough for child to ride on

Wagon

Wheelbarrow

Good Toys
for Two-Year-Olds

GENERAL

Boards for walking up inclines

Climbing apparatus with platform easily accessible

Jack-in-the-box

Kiddie Kar

Lego

Pegboards with large pegs in a variety of colors

Plastic animals

Play-Doh

Slide attached to climbing apparatus

Toy animals

THINGS FOR MAKE-BELIEVE

Dolls and doll accessories (blankets or colored cloth squares for covering beds and tables, bed, carriage, tea set)

Housekeeping materials, such as broom, unbreakable dishes, pots and pans, table, chairs, iron and ironing board, telephone

Wheeled vehicles, such as fire engine, cars, interlocking trains, trucks

Dress-up clothes, such as hats, high-heeled shoes, scarves, pocketbooks, dresses

TOYS FOR FINGER AND HAND ACTIVITY

Big beads to string

Books or toys that involve buttoning or lacing

Blocks

Rubber balls

Blackboard and chalk

Crayons, fingerpaints, clay

Toys for the
Two-and-a-Half-Year-Old

All the preceding
Boards for building, carrying, hauling, and walking
Clay
Fire truck, train, steam shovel, dump truck
Large hollow blocks
Large packing boxes

Large paintbrush for painting with water
Large wooden beads and string with long metal tip
Logs
Puzzles with big pieces
Screw toys
Soap-bubble pipe
Tricycle

Books for
Two-Year-Olds*

Bang, Molly. *Ten, Nine, Eight*. New York: Greenwillow, 1983.

Boynton, Sandra. *Moo Baa La La La*. New York: Simon & Schuster, 1984.

Brown, Margaret Wise. *Goodnight Moon*. New York: Harper & Row, 1947.

Burmingham, John. *Mr. Grumpy's Motor Car*. New York: Crowell, 1976.

Carle, Eric. *The Very Busy Spider*. New York: Philomel, 1969.

———. *The Very Hungry Caterpillar*. New York: Philomel, 1986.

Chorao, Kay. *Baby's Bed Time*. New York: Dutton, 1984.

Degen, Bruce. *Jamberry*. New York: HarperCollins, 1983.

Flack, Marjorie. *Ask Mr. Bear*. New York: Macmillan, 1971.

———. *Angus and the Cat*. New York: Doubleday, 1989.

Fox, Mem. *Time for Bed*. New York: Harcourt Brace Jovanovich, 1993.

Garland, Sarah. *All Gone*. New York: Puffin, 1991.

Hill, Eric. *Where's Spot?* New York: Putnam, 1980.

Hoban, Tana. *Of Colors and Things*. New York: Greenwillow, 1989.

Hughes, Shirley. *Two Shoes, New Shoes*. New York: Lothrop, 1986.

Kraus, Robert. *Goodnight, Richard Rabbit*. New York: Springfellow Dutton, 1972.

Kunhardt, Dorothy. *Pat the Bunny*. New York: Simon & Schuster, 1967.

Martin, Bill, Jr. *Brown Bear, Brown Bear*. New York: Holt, 1992.

Nichol, B. P., and Lobel, Anita. *Once a Lullaby*. New York: Morrow, 1992.

Shaw, Charles G. *It Looked Like Spilt Milk*. New York: HarperCollins, 1988.

*The authors acknowledge substantial help with this list from Nancy Dower.

Seuss, Dr. *The Cat in the Hat.* New York: Random House, 1957.

Tafuri, Nancy. *Early Morning in the Barn.* New York: Greenwillow, 1985.

————. *In a Red House.* New York: Greenwillow, 1987.

————. *My Friends.* New York: Greenwillow, 1987.

————. *Where We Sleep.* New York: Greenwillow, 1987.

Watanabe, Shigeo. *How Do I Put It On?* New York: Putnam, 1984.

————. *What a Good Lunch!* New York: Putnam, 1991.

————. *I Can Take a Walk.* New York: Putnam, 1991.

Wheeler, Cindy. *Marmalade's Nap.* New York: Knopf, 1983.

Williams, Sue. *I Went Walking.* New York: Harcourt Brace Jovanovich, 1989.

Books for the Parents of Two-Year-Olds

Alexander, Terry Pink. *Make Room for Twins*. New York: Bantam Books, 1987.

Ames, Louise Bates. *Parents Ask*. Syndicated newspaper column. New Haven, Conn.: Gesell Institute, 1952–

———. *What Do They Mean I'm Difficult?* Rosemont, N.J.: Programs for Education, 1986.

———. *Questions Parents Ask*. New York: Clarkson Potter, 1988.

Ames, Louise Bates, and Haber, Carol Chase. *He Hit Me First*. New York: Dembner/Warner, 1982.

Ames, Louise Bates, and Ilg, Frances L. *Your Three-Year-Old: Friend or Enemy*. New York: Delacorte, 1976.

Brazelton, T. Berry. *Toddlers and Parents*. New York: Delacorte, 1974.

Cuthbertson, Joanne, and Schevill, Susie. *Helping Your Child Sleep Through the Night*. New York: Doubleday, 1985.

Dodson, Fitzhugh. *How to Parent*. Los Angeles: Nash, 1970.

———. *How to Father*. Los Angeles: Nash, 1974.

———. *How to Grandparent*. New York: Harper & Row, 1981.

Feingold, Ben. *Why Your Child Is Hyperactive*. New York: Random House, 1975.

Ferber, Richard. *Solve Your Child's Sleep Problems*. New York: Simon & Schuster, 1985.

Hatfield, Antoinette, and Stanton, Peggy. *How to Help Your Child Eat Right*. Washington, D.C.: Acropolis Press, 1978.

Ilg, Frances L.; Ames, Louise Bates; and Baker, Sidney M. *Child Behavior*, rev. ed. New York: Harper & Row, 1981.

• *Appendix* •

Lansky, Vicky. *Best Practical Parenting Tips*. Deephaven, Minn.: Meadowlark Press, 1981.

Moore, Sheila, and Frost, Roon. *The Little Boy Book*. New York: Clarkson Potter, 1986.

Pitcher, Evelyn G., and Schultz, Lynn Hickey. *Boys and Girls at Play*. New York: Praeger Publishers, 1983.

Smith, Lendon. *Feed Your Kids Right*. New York: McGraw Hill, 1979.

Turecki, Stanley. *The Difficult Child*. New York: Bantam, 1989.

———— (with Sarah Wernick). *A Guide to the Emotional and Behavioral Problems of Normal Children*. New York: Bantam, 1991.

NOTES

1. A part of this description is adapted from Louise P. Woodcock's excellent but now out-of-print book, *Life and Ways of the Two-Year-Old* (New York: Basic Books, 1941).
2. Information about vision was supplied by Richard J. Apell, O.D., head of the Vision Department of the Gesell Institute of Child Development
3. Laurie Braga and Joseph Braga, *Learning and Growing: A Guide to Child Development* (Englewood Cliffs, N.J.: Prentice-Hall, 1975).
4. In order to set up and maintain a more or less controlled situation in which comparisons from child to child and from age to age are fair, our own observations were made during the course of the Gesell Preschool Examination, as described in *The First Five Years of Life*, by Arnold Gesell et al. (New York: Harper & Row, 1940). This examination was given individually to boys and girls of each of the preschool ages.
5. Some liberated women object to the phrase "Father's firm voice." The fact remains that, in general, fathers' voices are deeper and of a different, often more impressive, tonal quality than are mothers'.
6. T. Berry Brazelton, *Infants and Mothers* (New York: Delacorte, 1969).
7. Ben Feingold, *Why Your Child Is Hyperactive* (New York: Random House, 1974).

INDEX

Photo Credits

LOUISE BATES AMES

is a lecturer at the Yale Child Study Center and assistant professor emeritus at Yale University. She is co-founder of the Gesell Institute of Child Development and collaborator or co-author of three dozen of so books, including *The First Five Years of Life*, *Infant and Child in the Culture of Today*, *Child Rorschach Responses*, and the series *Your One-Year-Old* through *Your Ten- to Fourteen-Year-Old*. She has one child, three grandchildren, and four great-grandchildren.

FRANCES L. ILG

wrote numerous books, including *The Child from Five to Ten*, *Youth: The Years from Ten to Sixteen*, and *Child Behavior*, before her death in 1981. She was also a co-founder of the Gesell Institute of Child Development at Yale.